*New Library of Pastoral Care*
GENERAL EDITOR: DEREK BLOWS

Derek Blows is the Director of the Westminster Pastoral
Foundation, a psychotherapist at University College
Hospital, and a Professional Member of the Society of
Analytical Psychology. He is also an honorary canon of
Southwark Cathedral.

# Helping the Helpers

**Titles in this series include:**

*Still Small Voice: An Introduction to Counselling*
MICHAEL JACOBS

*Letting Go: Caring for the Dying and Bereaved*
PETER SPECK AND IAN AINSWORTH-SMITH

*Living Alone: The Inward Journey to Fellowship*
MARTIN ISRAEL

*Invisible Barriers: Pastoral Care with Physically Disabled People*
JESSIE VAN DONGEN-GARRAD

*Learning to Care: Christian Reflection on Pastoral Practice*
MICHAEL H. TAYLOR

*Liberating God: Private Care and Public Struggle*
PETER SELBY

*Make or Break: An Introduction to Marriage Counselling*
JACK DOMINIAN

*Meaning in Madness: The Pastor and the Mentally Ill*
JOHN FOSKETT

*Paid to Care?: The Limits of Professionalism in Pastoral Care*
ALASTAIR V. CAMPBELL

*Swift to Hear: Facilitating Skills in Listening and Responding*
MICHAEL JACOBS

*Brief Encounters: Pastoral Ministry through the Occasional Offices*
WESLEY CARR

*Love the Stranger: Ministry in Multi-Faith Areas*
ROGER HOOKER AND CHRISTOPHER LAMB

*Being There: Pastoral Care in Time of Illness*
PETER SPECK

*Going Somewhere: People with Mental Handicaps and their Pastoral Care*
SHEILA HOLLINS AND MARGARET GRIMER

*Made in Heaven?: Ministry with Those Intending Marriage*
PETER CHAMBERS

*Family Matters: The Pastoral Care of Personal Relationships*
SUE WALROND-SKINNER

*Helping the Helpers: Supervision and Pastoral Care*
JOHN FOSKETT AND DAVID LYALL

*The Pastor as Theologian: The Integration of Pastoral Ministry,
Theology and Discipleship*
WESLEY CARR

*City of God? Pastoral Care in the Inner City*
NICHOLAS BRADBURY

*Clergy Stress: The Hidden Conflicts in Ministry*
MARY ANNE COATE

*Holding in Trust: The Appraisal of Ministry*
MICHAEL JACOBS

*A Dictionary of Pastoral Care*
edited by ALASTAIR V. CAMPBELL

*New Library of Pastoral Care*
GENERAL EDITOR: DEREK BLOWS

# HELPING THE HELPERS

*Supervision and Pastoral Care*

## John Foskett and David Lyall

First published in Great Britain 1988
SPCK
Holy Trinity Church
Marylebone Road
London NW1 4DU

Third impression 1990

British Library Cataloguing in Publication Data

Foskett, John
   Helping the helpers : supervision and
   pastoral care.
   1. Christian church. Pastoral work — Manuals
   I. Title    II. Lyall, David   III. Series
   253

   ISBN 0-281-04386-8

Filmset by Pioneer
Printed in Great Britain by
Courier International Ltd, Tiptree

# Contents

# Foreword

The *New Library of Pastoral Care* has been planned to meet
the needs of those people concerned with pastoral care,
whether clergy or lay, who seek to improve their knowledge
and skills in this field. Equally, it is hoped that it may prove
useful to those secular helpers who may wish to understand
the role of the pastor.

Pastoral care in every age has drawn from contemporary
secular knowledge to inform its understanding of man and
his various needs and of the ways in which these needs might
be met. Today it is perhaps the secular helping professions of
social work, counselling and psychotherapy, and community
development which have particular contributions to make to
the pastor in his work. Such knowledge does not stand still,
and a pastor would have a struggle to keep up with the
endless tide of new developments which pour out from these
and other disciplines, and to sort out which ideas and
practices might be relevant to his particular pastoral needs.
Among present-day ideas, for instance, of particular value
might be an understanding of the social context of the pastoral
task, the dynamics of the helping relationship, the attitudes
and skills as well as factual knowledge which might make for
effective pastoral intervention and, perhaps most significant
of all, the study of particular cases, whether through verbatim
reports of interviews or general case presentation. The
discovery of ways of learning from what one is doing is
becoming increasingly important.

There is always a danger that a pastor who drinks deeply
at the well of a secular discipline may lose his grasp of his
own pastoral identity and become 'just another' social worker
or counsellor. It in no way detracts from the value of these
professions to assert that the role and task of the pastor are
quite unique among the helping professions and deserve to be

clarified and strengthened rather than weakened. The theological commitment of the pastor and the appropriate use of his role will be a recurrent theme of the series. At the same time the pastor cannot afford to work in a vacuum. He needs to be able to communicate and co-operate with those helpers in other disciplines whose work may overlap, without loss of his own unique role. This in turn will mean being able to communicate with them through some understanding of their concepts and language.

Finally, there is a rich variety of styles and approaches in pastoral work within the various religious traditions. No attempt will be made to secure a uniform approach. The Library will contain the variety, and even perhaps occasional eccentricity, which such a title suggests. Some books will be more specifically theological and others more concerned with particular areas of need or practice. It is hopes that all of them will have a usefulness that will reach right across the boundaries of religious denomination.

DEREK BLOWS
*Series Editor*

# Preface

This book has been written in the belief that the time is ripe for an exploration of the theories and methods of training and supporting all those who exercise a ministry of pastoral care within the Church. This statement sets both the horizons and the boundaries of the enterprise. It is not simply a book about training students in pastoral care, though that of course is involved; rather, it recognises that, speaking theologically, pastoral care is a ministry of the whole people of God and that in practice this is exercised by many in the Church, both ordained and lay. It is further recognised that those of us who seek to help others, need some kind of help ourselves, not just before we begin helping, but as an integral part of all our ministry. We hope therefore that the ideas in this book will be of help to a wide spectrum of people within the Church. We hope also that people outside the Church will find something of value too (though we find it hard to draw lines). Nevertheless we write from within the context of faith, believing that 'pastoral supervision' raises questions peculiar to itself, especially in relation to the dialogue between the Christian faith and the human sciences.

The authors do not claim to be saying anything fundamentally new. It is a book about supervision: a concept and a practice which has been extensively discussed in other contexts. For many years supervision has been regarded as an essential component of the training and professional support of social workers, psychotherapists and counsellors of many kinds. In theological education it has been a cornerstone in the development of Clinical Pastoral Education in North America during the last forty or so years. Yet books on supervision relating to the 'secular' helping professions have not addressed issues specific to pastoral education; neither is there readily available one book which gathers together the material presented in this volume.

Both authors were engaged in the practice of supervision and had begun to write separately when asked to join forces by Derek Blows. The response to this suggestion, on the part of both of us, was a somewhat hesitant 'Yes', for while we have much in common we are two very different people. Both of us have had parish experience, one in the Church of England, the other in the Church of Scotland; both of us have been full-time hospital chaplains for a number of years, one in a psychiatric hospital, the other mainly in general hospitals; both of us have had experience of supervising students on placement; we knew one another through our involvement in various pastoral care organisations. Yet knowing one another we knew we were different people and, as it happened, this shaped our approach to working on the book; one of us likes to start with experience and then to move towards the formulation of ideas, while the other freely admits to a desire to contain the chaos of experience within some kind of provisional conceptual structure (those who know us will recognise which of us is which!). Yet acknowledging this tension and working with it was of value because it is the very tension which is inherent in any attempt to reflect upon pastoral care and upon education for that ministry. Where should we begin? This was the question we asked ourselves once we had assembled the material we wished to present in the book. We could, at least logically, have started at points other than the one we chose: perhaps with our understanding of the nature of pastoral care which we set out in Chapter 7, or even by describing the practicalities of supervision which we place in the last chapter. Yet we have begun with case material and introduced theory and reflection as we have gone along, for our central thesis is that if we do not learn by reflecting on experience we do not learn at all. In that sense a book about pastoral supervision can by its very nature be of only limited value. Nevertheless we offer it as an introduction to the subject, not as a complete guidebook but as a map of the territory. We hope people will take from it what is of value to them and set it alongside their own experience of caring and being cared for. We have enjoyed working together. We have argued over many things but it has been fun.

We are grateful to many people who have helped us. Alastair Campbell was a prime instigator for David Lyall and has continued to provide much appreciated support and comment on various parts of the manuscript, as have John Patton and Gillian Morton. For John Foskett the staff, Robin McGlashan, Regina Allen, Cathy Crawford, Jean Thompson, Ian Ainsworth-Smith and Tom Leary, and the participants on the Supervision and Consultation Course at the Maudsley Hospital have regularly encouraged, and sometimes forced, him to develop and articulate his ideas on this subject.

We wish to express our appreciation to the many people who have allowed us to use their stories, albeit reworked and adapted by us, in the early chapters of this book. We are also grateful to those who have provided much-needed secretarial help: Karen Morton, Mary Donaldson and Moya Southgate. Above all we wish to thank our wives Mary and Margaret not only for their support during the writing of this book, but as those who have most surely provided 'help for the helpers' in both ministry and marriage.

# ONE

# New Developments in Pastoral Care

Pastoral care has always been a characteristic of the life of the Church. It is care for persons rooted in the Christian tradition, a feature of the common life of those who claim allegiance to the Church, and involving many who would not number themselves within its fellowship. The form which this pastoral care has taken has varied from one historical epoch to another.

In their classic history of pastoral care Clebsch and Jaekle offer the following definition:

> The ministry of the cure of souls or pastoral care consists of helping acts done by representative Christian persons directed towards the healing, sustaining, guiding and reconciling of troubled persons whose troubles arise in the context of ultimate meanings and concerns.[1]

Clebsch and Jaekle demonstrate how the dominant mode of pastoral care has been a response to the needs of the Church at different times in its history: sustaining in the early days when it was believed that this world would come to an end, reconciling in times of persecution when many believers abandoned their faith, healing during the sacramentalism of the high Middle Ages, and guidance during the voluntaryism of the nineteenth century.

In the first half of this century an answer to the question 'What is pastoral care?' would have been easily forthcoming. The phrase was a full and adequate description of certain transactions which took place between a minister or priest and members of his congregation or parish. The words described what happened when he (the masculine form is used deliberately) visited the sick, comforted the bereaved, responded to family crises and went about the many other duties among 'his' people which symbolised, indeed manifested, God's concern for them. The training needed for this task could be described in comparatively simple terms. It was part of the discipline of Practical Theology, defined as

> the discipline concerned with the offering of advice, techniques and the fruits of long experience by those long-established in the ministry to those intending to enter it. Clearly the main requirement for a practical theologian — apart from an adequate grounding in general theology — was considered to be extensive parochial experience.[2]

In recent years this view of pastoral care and of the training required has undergone extensive modification. The rapidly developing psychosocial sciences have helped us to understand better the complexities of the human personality and of the nature of helping relationships. Pastoral care and education have not remained immune from these influences. It has come to be recognised that the well-intentioned giving of advice is not an adequate response to the problems of living experienced by men and women. The insights of anthropology, psychology and sociology, which have had an impact on other areas of professional education, have also affected education for pastoral care.[3]

Furthermore, our understanding of ministry itself has changed. While many would still consider a solitary minister in his parish to be the norm, this model now coexists alongside a much wider variety of ministries. Some denominations have not yet ordained women, but even when denied the opportunity of presiding at sacramental worship women are fully involved in pastoral ministry, bringing their complementary insights to caring for people. One incumbent to a single parish is no longer the invariable rule, with congregations often grouped together and leadership provided by a team of ministers. Such teams vary enormously in their composition. They may be ecumenical in nature or include non-stipendiary or auxiliary ministers, that is, ministers who share fully in liturgical and pastoral leadership but who are not paid for the work they do.[4] Sometimes, too, the members of team ministries may be paid but not ordained to the ministry of word and sacrament, for instance, deaconesses, social workers or youth and community workers.

Further, the past three decades have seen a remarkable expansion of the work of ordained ministry in non-parochial and secular settings. The pastoral role of hospital chaplains, both full-time and part-time, is an obvious example, and this is also prominent in the work of chaplains in industry, the forces, prisons, educational institutions and the arts. Many non-stipendiary ministers see their main sphere of influence as being at their place of work rather than in the local congregation.

Most significant of all has been the emphasis in all denominations on the importance of lay pastoral care, and the ministry of the whole people of God. This has always been part of the ethos of many branches of the Church, for example, through elders in the Reformed tradition, class leaders in the Methodist Church and churchwardens in the Anglican communion. The theological and practical importance of this is now being affirmed anew in all denominations and the need for training for such work recognised.[5] The central thrust of the rapidly expanding Theological Education by Extension movement is to equip God's people for ministry and its educational philosophy has much in common with new approaches to pastoral education.

A growing number of attempts to wrest the whole enterprise of pastoral care from its traditional moorings have left it firmly attached to the biblical, but no less paternalistic, metaphor of shepherd and sheep. This has tended to produce a kind of ecclesiastical casework in which a few are always the workers and the rest the cases. As other professions have sought to examine and change the unhealthy, dependent and collusive relationship between helper and helped, so the more sociologically and politically aware theologians have encouraged the Church to re-examine the pastoral metaphor. In St John's Gospel of course there is only one shepherd and many sheep. This has traditionally been interpreted as the model for each congregation, in which there will be a shepherd and lots of sheep, but to divide out the roles and functions in this way is to miss the point of our mutuality and interdependence within the one body and one fold. Alastair Campbell has been

*Helping the Helpers*

particularly forthright in exposing the dubious nature of our theological authority for this traditional view of pastoral care.[6]

In its place has come a less individually focused and problem-based pastoral care, and a more corporate and interdependent approach which acknowledges the significance of groups, systems and organisations as well as individuals, and strengths as well as weaknesses. A major influence in this direction has been that of the late R. A. Lambourne, an Anglican doctor who studied theology and became one of the founders of the Diploma in Pastoral Studies at Birmingham University. After surveying trends in both Britain and the United States, he became convinced that pastoral care was in danger of taking a wrong turning, that pastoral counselling was coming to be recognised as the normative mode of pastoral care and that such pastoral counselling was itself defective in its philosophy.

> My thesis is that the pastoral counselling called for in this country during the next twenty years cannot be built around a practice and conceptual framework derived from professional problem-solving and prevention of breakdown. . . . What is required is a pastoral care which is lay, corporate, adventurous, variegated and diffuse.[7]

He felt that current developments in pastoral counselling were based on a medical model of helping, with its roots in secular psychotherapy, and on a philosophy and practice in which the supreme value was the 'elimination of defect', rather than on the building up of a community of faith, hope and love in which women and men were enabled to attain their full potential as human beings.

> Not the prevention of illness, nor the removal of illness, but a corporate vision and excitement which enable the participant people to responsibly accept and transform a supra-normal level of anxiety into the stuff of health and freedom is the concept of pastoral care and mental health we need to press.[8]

All these developments have contributed in a somewhat haphazard way to the practice of ministry and pastoral care within the Churches. We say 'haphazard' because there have been so few attempts to integrate these ideas and developments with one another or within training programmes for those to be ordained or licensed as pastors of the whole people of God.

So it is that we find the traditional view of pastoral care floating uneasily alongside a more contemporary view. In one parish a call from the vicar is worth two from the curate and any number from the laity; and in another priest and people devise and practice a system of mutual care, in which all share in the preparation for sacraments, community care and social and political action. In the absence of a more systematic integration of traditional and contemporary developments in the theory and practice of pastoral care, it is still possible to see the different ways in which the training and development of pastors is being influenced.

1. The traditional apprentice model mentioned earlier remains the most common model for pastoral training, and it has been extended to incorporate many of the new developments. Candidates for ordination and licensing are expected to learn from the experience of being with and working alongside more experienced craftsmen and -women, both in parishes and congregations, and in more specialist environments such as hospitals, prisons and community agencies.

2. Following developments in our contemporary understanding of human interaction there has been a rapid growth in human relations training. Courses in the skills of relating, caring and counselling abound. Some are generic, emphasising helping skills, while others specialise, for instance, in bereavement counselling. At the most fundamental and basic level, the skills of attending, listening and responding are the raw material of all care, and students of pastoral care are being encouraged to learn and practice these skills in their work.

3. At the academic level has come the development of Practical and Pastoral Theology. From lay ministry courses to university diplomas in Pastoral Studies, more and more people have entered into the intellectual task of relating faith and life to one another, and then of applying the fruits of that

integration to the practice of ministry in contemporary society.

4. For many of those involved in one or more of the above, the tension of the traditional and the contemporary, and of relating faith to life and theory to practice, has inevitably taken its personal toll emotionally and spiritually. The human growth, personal counselling and spiritual direction movements all contribute to help would-be pastors learn the fundamental lesson of accepting help and care for themselves, while developing their pastoral and professional identity.

An integrated approach to pastoral care and education will reflect the influence of all of these four training methods at some time or other. The common element in all of them is a relationship. In the first it is the relationship between master and apprentice, in the others between expert and novice, teacher and pupil, counsellor and client. In each one a relationship is the context in which learning takes place. It is within a partnership that knowledge is imparted, experience compared, skills perfected, practice assessed and insight nurtured. Furthermore there is another kind of relationship involved, that between the participants and their task: the apprentice/master and the craft, the novice/expert and the skills, the pupil/teacher and the knowledge, and the client/counsellor and the insight. It is the relationship in each case which contains the process of change, growth and development, together with all the attendant pressures and anxieties. Like the potter's hands around the clay, the relationship gives shape to the creation by holding all the material together while it is in the making.

## Supervision

The supervisory relationship is one which aims to embrace something of all the elements and influences mentioned above, and to integrate them as effectively as possible. We believe it can make a major and unique contribution to the training and support of pastors, just as it has in the development of other training professions. In the following chapters we will attempt to show how the relationship and process of supervision works, how it draws upon the relationships mentioned above and how it integrates and extends them. We will do this by describing and then exploring the stories of some supervisory relationships, looking first from within them to see how the participants function, and how they use their relationship in the service of their work together. At the same time we will introduce one by one the most important theories about supervision, and illustrate them by reference to the same stories. Important as supervision is in the preparation for, and the early years of, ministry, such are the demands upon pastors today that it is best to plan for it as an essential support for all who offer pastoral care throughout their ministry. In Chapter 6 on consultation we explore this aspect of supervision further. In Chapter 7 we review the current assumptions and tensions of pastoral care which in one way or another affect the work of supervision. And in Chapters 8 and 9 we look at more of the theories and practicalities of supervision.

## Notes

1. Clebsch, W., and Jaekle, C. R., *Pastoral Care in Historical Perspective,* New York: Harper Torchbooks 1967, p. 4.
2. Gill, R., 'The Future of Practical Theology', *Contact* 56, 1977: 1, p. 17.
3. Pattison, S., 'The Use of the Behavioural Sciences in Pastoral Studies' in Ballard, P. (ed.), *The Foundations of Pastoral Studies and Practical Theology,* University College Cardiff 1987, pp. 79–85.
4. Hodge, M., *Non-Stipendiary Ministry in the Church of England,* CIO 1983; Baelz, P., and Jacob, W., *Ministers of the Kingdom: Explorations in Non-Stipendiary Ministry,* CIO 1985.
5. Kinsler, F. Ross, *Ministry by the People,* Geneva: World Council of Churches 1983.
6. Campbell, A., *The Rediscovery of Pastoral Care,* Darton, Longman and Todd 1981.
7. Lambourne, R. A., 'Objections to a National Pastoral Organisation' *Contact* 35, June 1971, p. 26.
8. Ibid., p. 27.

# TWO

# Learning how to Learn

In its simplest form pastoral supervision has been defined as 'a method of doing and reflecting on ministry'. It has an active and a passive component represented graphically thus:

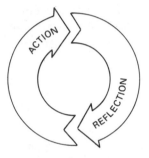

The learner *acts* in some way, offering pastoral care by visiting a parishioner, leading a discussion group or preparing a couple for marriage. The supervisor helps the learner *reflect* critically upon that action when they meet together. Reflection of course involves both the intelligence and the imagination. In our first example below, the story of a theological student with an experienced minister, we will adopt the minister's own technique and concentrate upon the latter. We invite our readers to join us in using their imagination as a most effective instrument for stimulating the process of action and reflection.

Ian was a final-year theological student who, as part of his preparation for the ordained ministry, was attached to a local congregation sharing in its life and worship. Each week he was expected to undertake some pastoral visits. On one occasion the minister asked him to call on Mrs Brown a 55-year-old lady whose husband had died suddenly six weeks previously. Ian wasn't looking forward to this visit—he had little personal experience of bereavement—and kept putting it off as long as possible. Eventually, however, he plucked up courage to knock on Mrs Brown's door, and found himself ushered into the front room. At first Mrs Brown seemed very bright and cheerful, and showed great interest in Ian's studies and plans for the future. Nothing was said about her recent loss until Ian took a deep breath and said, 'And how have things been with you these past six weeks?' Mrs Brown broke down and cried for several minutes. Ian felt totally inadequate. Not knowing what to say he sat there feeling helpless and embarrassed while she wept. Feeling he should do something he said, 'Would you like me to say a prayer before I leave?' To which Mrs Brown replied 'Yes, if you like'. Ian prayed and left quickly.

When he met with Hamish the minister the following week, Ian was encouraged to talk about what had happened during his visit to Mrs Brown, a visit which he felt had gone badly wrong. He was able to acknowledge his anxieties before the visit, his feelings of helplessness during the visit and the reasons why he offered to say a prayer. Together Ian and Hamish tried to understand what was happening both to Ian and Mrs Brown; they looked at the different ways in which Ian might have responded to the situation, and began to make plans for future visits to Mrs Brown and others like her.

As a theological student in his last year of training prior to ordination, Ian is in the process of transition from study and preparation to the practice of ministry itself, from the role of a learner who is often dependent on others to that of a minister on whom others mostly depend. What is more, he is in the midst of a trial run, an opportunity to practise the work he is going to do, and to try himself out in his new role. On the surface this appears to be a very straightforward and useful experience, and yet if we put ourselves in Ian's shoes it is not difficult to experience his uncertainty, excitement and anxiety. At last he has the chance to test his vocation, but also he is exposing himself to the possibility that he has chosen wrongly, or that others will find him wanting and

unfit for ministry. Such ruminations and no doubt many
others will accompany him, rather like background music.
The more uncomfortable the sounds, the more Ian, like all of
us, will try to turn the volume down. The experience he has
will also affect the volume, and we can guess that much of his
time and energy will be taken up in managing that 'volume
control'. Keeping in mind this imaginative leap into Ian's
shoes and experience let's follow him into the visit he made.

First he was, we learn, *expected* to do some visits.
Expectations are important and two-sided. On the one hand
to have things expected of us can help us feel needed and
valued, and enhance our belief in our usefulness. On the
other hand, expectations can be a burden, an obligation we
cannot live up to, and unrealistic expectations can undermine
our confidence and sense of value. Hamish can seem to be
both a patron and a judge. The story makes it clear that Ian
felt up to his minister's expectations on the whole, but unsure
in relation to his visit to Mrs Brown. The thought of that
affected the 'volume control' so much that he put the visit off
and turned down the sound of his anxiety about it. It is not
difficult to imagine Ian's feelings standing on Mrs Brown's
doorstep and his rising anxiety as he waits for her to open the
door: perhaps she will be out and it won't be his fault that he
has not seen her yet. She is not out but her behaviour eases
his fear; *she* takes care of him. Her interest gives value to
what Ian has already done and what he is now deliberating
about. At the moment when Ian expected to feel most
inadequate, Mrs Brown helps him recall both what he has
done and is planning to do. We can imagine Ian growing in
stature as he tells his story, so much so that he finds the
strength to broach the subject he has come about. Thus
encouraged Mrs Brown breaks down or perhaps more
accurately breaks through to her distress, and shares it with
Ian in the most natural way. Something about her feelings
and his presence enables her to go on doing what she needs to
do for several minutes. Ian's 'volume control' is of course
affected, but he manages to control his sense of inadequacy
and embarrassment sufficiently to sit there helplessly. Such
moments are at the core of pastoral care. At this distance
from the story it is easy to see how helpful and necessary it
was for Mrs Brown to let out her distress and misery, and to

have Ian take upon himself some of the weight of her feelings: her sense of helplessness and inadequacy and possible embarrassment too. Of course Ian does not realise he is doing that for her, or that his helplessness is, in fact, an asset that prevents him from interfering with what Mrs Brown is doing. Eventually his anxiety gets the better of his helpful inadequacy, and he interferes as a way of 'turning the volume down' for himself. Mrs Brown sensing that the prayer is more for him than her encourages him to go ahead, if that is what he wants. He lets her cry and she lets him pray, each shares, and so bears, some of the anxiety of the other.

The story makes it clear that very little of this, if anything, is available to Ian. This experience of trying himself out as a minister will help and teach him very little on its own. If, for instance, Ian had had no minister to turn to, or if he had not been able to bring himself to tell the story of what happened, then at best the experience would have been discarded as a failure or at worst incorporated into the sounds of the background music. Ian however did have a colleague to return to and was able to share his experience as an essential prelude to learning from it. Hamish began this process by inviting Ian to talk about what had happened. Telling the story of a visit step by step and as descriptively as possible is the best way of bringing the story back to life. The minister's interest and his lack of censorship or judgement all contribute to the effectiveness of Ian's sharing.

As Ian speaks a picture unfolds and the sounds of the background music begin to come through: the visit going badly wrong, the anticipatory fears, the sense of helplessness, the feelings which led to the offer of a prayer. The minister's interest and non-judgemental attitude allows Ian to 'turn the volume up', and to get some of the anxiety off his chest. Once relieved, he is free to look afresh at what happened. Perhaps Hamish might have encouraged Ian to use his imagination to get inside Mrs Brown's feelings regarding what went on during the visit:

— what it meant to have lost her husband;
— how difficult the last few months must have been for her;
— whether she and her husband had been able to face together the fact that he was not going to get better;

— how she might have felt about being visited by a student rather than by the minister;

— the reason why she kept talking so brightly, asking Ian about his future plans and avoiding discussion of her own situation;

— why she broke down when Ian broached the subject;

— the possible reasons for her obvious embarrassment when Ian offered to pray with her.

Our exercise in imagination has therefore taken us first of all into a consideration of what might have been happening to Ian as a person, and secondly into some reflection about what may have been happening during this pastoral visit. Pohly describes supervision as having two foci: the person in supervision and the ministry which he or she performs. Obviously these cannot be separated and must indeed overlap. Pohly represents this situation in the following diagram:[1]

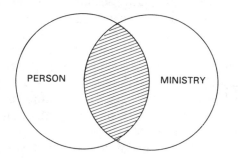

It is the area of overlap between 'person' and 'ministry' which is the focus of supervision. Hamish as supervisor will be particularly concerned about the interaction between who Ian is as a person, in all his uniqueness, and how Ian functions in ministry. The supervisory task is to allow Ian to become sufficiently free to look afresh at what happened, to see and take from his experience insights which will be valuable to him in future ministry. Some of these insights are likely to be more accessible than others, but all can in time contribute to Ian's learning, his practice of ministry and his identity as a pastor. This is the most basic model of supervision, the 'Action-Reflection' model. A person engages in ministry, steps back in order to reflect upon it, and returns to ministry with fresh insights, to return later for further reflection. The supervisory task flows between action and reflection. In the situation under consideration Ian has come to Hamish to discuss his visit to Mrs Brown and together they reflect upon that visit. Hopefully Ian will gain insights which will help him in future visits to Mrs Brown or in other situations of ministry which in turn will form the starting point for future supervision.

The process of acting and then reflecting on that action is therefore one which needs repeating again and again. The more experience Ian has, the more help he will get to apply his learning and to have it confirmed by the greater effectiveness of his practice. There is of course far more to this process than the free use of one's imagination, but that is an essential element. Without it much of any experience will be either lost or so rigidly ordered that only premature and partial conclusions are drawn from it. In the next chapter we will show how imagination and intellect are related and brought to bear upon experience.

## Note

1. Pohly, K. H., *Pastoral Supervision,* Institute of Religion, Texas Medical Centre, Houston, 1977, p. 66.

THREE

# Learning and Experience

In the last chapter we saw how Ian was helped by his minister to reflect on his visit to Mrs Brown. Left to himself it is probable that he would have learnt very little. Learning from experience is not inevitable. In our dealings with people we often find ourselves repeating the mistakes we thought we had overcome, for our experience can reinforce bad habits as easily as it can help us develop good ones. Supervision provides us with more than the opportunity to reflect on our actions one by one. It also gives us the chance to discover how we learn, how we use experience to hinder as well as help us. As we use experience in either one way or the other, it is essential for us to know how we use it. Another model of supervision illustrates this process of learning how we learn.

**Learning from Experience — a Model of Supervision**

This model, originally derived from theories of learning amongst adults,[1] extends the simple process of action and reflection to a four-phase sequence, in which each phase arises out of the one preceding it.

We make the most of learning from experience if we can observe all the phases and their sequence, and if we can develop the habit of repeating the sequence. Learning rarely takes place as easily and systematically as any theory suggests; nevertheless we will apply this one first to the work of Ian and his supervisor, and then more extensively to that of John, another student, and his supervisor.

14

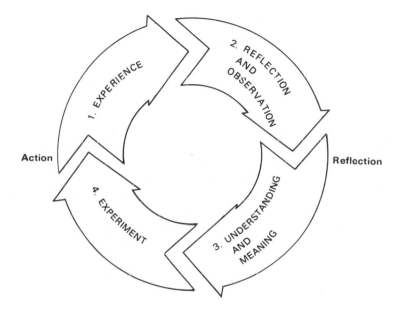

*Phase 1: Experience*
*What actually happened.*

Ian's attachment to this church provides him with the experience of being in a placement, his visit to Mrs Brown is an experience within that placement, and her breakdown is a critical incident within the visit. Any experience, whether brief or prolonged, can teach us something. The experiences which are the most fruitful are those which stay with us, stirring our feelings and occupying our thoughts. Because they disturb or excite us they are the ones that can motivate us to learn. We can capitalise on our anxiety or our interest, and put it to work for us. Ian found his visit to Mrs Brown to be that kind of experience. He was worried about it, and was glad to have the chance to talk. His supervisor was alert to this need and encouraged him to begin by explaining 'what *happened*'. He got Ian to recall and represent the actual events of his visit, the experience itself first.

*Phase 2: Reflection and Observation*

Reflecting upon the experience and its effect.

We invited you to use your imagination to enter into the characters of those involved in Ian's visit and the supervision. That is one very effective way of reflecting broadly and inclusively about experience. It helps us to suspend judgement, to allow us to ponder and wonder about anything that comes to mind or evokes feelings. Ian was able to do this: to acknowledge how anxious he felt about the visit, how relieved he was to talk about his own plans and hopes, and how this gave him courage to ask Mrs Brown about herself. He is supported by the minister's recognition of these feelings, and his interest in, rather than judgement of, them. Without that support Ian could have dried up, passing over his panic and embarrassment in an attempt to put the whole visit behind him, write it off and start again. Difficult and disturbing experiences can easily reinforce a sense of failure.

*Phase 3: Understanding and Meaning*

Understanding the experience and its effect and discovering something of its meaning.

Once Ian had told his story and shared his sense of failure he was free of some of the emotional weight. He was able to begin to think about what happened, and to see how far his own feelings obscured other things about the visit: — Mrs Brown's caring for him, her chance to show her feelings openly for the first time and to be comforted by his presence. Perhaps these thoughts began to strike chords with what he had learnt at college: — the sharing of burdens within the body of Christ, the mutuality of ministry and pastoral care, his own suffering in his helplessness as an instrument of ministry to her, his prayer of panic, the expression of a need, and a belief in the presence and dependability of God. Just as the reflection phase can be like an act of repentance, so this phase, if it is creative, has the quality of a revelation, bringing new light and understanding to replace the sense of fear and failure. The experience and understanding of others, whether in the doctrines and theology of the Church or in the theories of the human sciences, are now beginning to be available to Ian to help him place his experience in a wider context, and bring his intellectual understanding to bear on his work, so that each plays upon the other.

### Phase 4: Experiment

Preparing for future experiences.

The search for meaning and its discovery enables connections to be made between theory and practice. Ian and the minister discuss what Ian said and did and what he might have said and done, the many alternative responses that he could have made, making it clear that there is not just one but many equally valid ways of caring. They look forward too and anticipate what Ian's next visit might be like, his hopes and fears, and consider what Ian could take from this experience to help him in his future ministry.

This model of learning has been applied and researched in many different fields, and is useful in demonstrating not only how learning is facilitated effectively, but also how it is hindered by the omission or over-emphasis of any of the four phases. We all have preferences in our use of experience. 'Doers' relish new experiences, but have less inclination to reflect upon and understand the significance of what happens to them. 'Thinkers', on the other hand, prefer to collect all the facts to brood upon, sift and analyse. Learning from experience is distorted by these preferences. Likewise the environment, context and culture within which we work can favour one phase more than another. Ian was moving from an academic environment in his college to a practical one in the parish, where his minister had been working for many years. Each is likely to be more at home in a different phase of the sequence. Ian we know was uneasy in the face of death and bereavement, and yet that was where Mrs Brown was. With this model in mind the supervisor can begin to detect the way in which Ian learns, and how to help him make more of the phases that he finds difficult.

The story of Ian and his minister illustrated how the sequence of experience and reflection, thinking and understanding, anticipating and experimenting can help learning take place and can be applied in practice. Now we will look more closely at this process in the work of another student preparing for the ministry, and his supervisor in a general hospital where he was on placement. This story demonstrates how the under- or over-emphasis of any of the phases can distort learning, and so affect practice. In our experience this is inevitable in supervision, particularly in the early stages of the work, when student and supervisor are new to one another and need time to build up a working relationship. It also shows how central the relationship is to supervision, and how the tension between supervisor and student can generate the energy for learning. Too much tension and the relationship can break, too little and there is no impetus at all. In this way the distortions and deviations which naturally occur are vital and can be used to good effect as the relationship develops.

John chose this particular placement because of an interest he had in working with the elderly. We will follow the supervision through the first four meetings, which happened in each of the first four weeks of the placement. The supervisor recorded what took place.

**First meeting**

(S = Supervisor; J = John)

S1:   Well John, how is the placement going?
J1:   All right, I suppose.
S2:   What do you mean, 'I suppose'. That sounds a bit ambivalent.
J2:   Well, I genuinely enjoy old folk, but they can be very demanding.
S3:   Demanding?
J3:   Well, they just keep telling you the same old story every time you go in, and they expect you to sit and listen.
S4:   You find that difficult?
J4:   Well, yes . . . but you have to be kind to them. It's just the way I've been brought up, I suppose.

S5: Brought up? You sound as though you have experience of old folk.

J5: Yes, we always had one of my grandparents staying with us.

S6: Always?

J6: Yes, as long as I can remember, we had at least one of them in the house. Mum and Dad were very good to them and we were expected to be the same.

S7: Having grandparents around all the time can sometimes be a bit of a strain.

J7: Funny you should say that . . . Yes, it was sometimes . . . sometimes got Mum and Dad down . . . Sometimes after we kids went to bed they had terrible rows . . . Each felt an obligation to look after their own . . . but they seemed to resent the demands of the other. Looking back, we had no real privacy as a family. We never had a family holiday together.

S8: Did it affect you in other ways . . . you personally?

J8: Well, you know . . . the record-player had to be kept low . . . and it wasn't easy to have friends in.

S9: So on the one hand you were taught to respect your grandparents . . . and on the other hand, you came to realise what a strain it put on your family's life.

J9: That's right! I really felt mad with the old folk sometimes . . . but it wasn't as simple as that because there was a lot of genuine love around as well.

S10: And that's maybe part of the reason why you want to work with old folk?

J10: I hadn't thought of that . . . But I find it so hard to cope with some of the old folk on the ward. Some of them are super, but others just witter on and on without any reason to what they say.

S11: It's difficult to tolerate them or to see why they do it.

J11: I suppose that's all they've got left to do.

S12: Well maybe there's more to it than that. Why don't you have a look at what Ronald Blythe has written? *The View in Winter*[2] has a lot about old people and their stories.

J12: Right, I'll dip into that this week.

Reading this account of their conversation in the light of the sequence we have in mind reveals a number of things.

*Phase 1: Experience*

Although it is alluded to, John's experience in the placement never really comes alive in the meeting. He says nothing about what he actually did or said to anyone on the ward. Instead he talks in an emotional but very general way *about*, rather than *of*, his experience. He finds the elderly very demanding, and finds listening to their stories over and over again unsatisfying. And yet he gives no account of any of the stories, no picture of how the demands were made. Phase 1 is passed over, hidden beneath his feelings about it.

*Phase 2: Reflection*

What is more, the supervisor is drawn immediately into the reflection phase, and joins John in exploring his feelings rather than the experience which has provoked them. This in turn leads them away from the placement and back into John's life story, which he describes far more graphically. As it happens this reveals something of significance. John grew up amidst the strains and stresses of a three-generational household. He learnt about 'love' and 'hate' in families from his early experience and, in particular, to acknowledge the positive and reject the negative. Unlike his parents he had no obvious object for the latter, since both grandparents were equally his. Now in his placement he has found objects for both feelings and cannot deny them, even though it feels wrong. This is an important exploration, as it reveals so much about John's motivation for pastoral work, and how he learnt from his early and formative life experience. The more we know about what motivates us to care for others, the more control we can have over our needs and wishes for them, and the less we will impose upon them. All of us, like John, are prone to use our work to resolve those things which were unresolved in our early lives. Valuable as this digression into John's family history was, it nevertheless distorted the supervision, and John's learning from it. It would have been better for the supervisor to have explored these things with John prior to the placement at a preliminary interview, but as so often happens the work itself exposes the personal issues which have remained dormant for so long. The supervisor sensing this digression tries to get back on course by linking John's personal story to his wish to work with the elderly. However, the interpretation is premature and lost on John, who is still immersed in his ambivalence towards the elderly.

## Phase 3: Understanding and Meaning

The student and supervisor will be affected by the feelings aroused between them in the reflection phase, particularly if those feelings are difficult and uncomfortable. They will want to resolve the difficulty and alleviate the discomfort, and this need will provide them with the motivation to search for some understanding. At its most productive this can lead to a real grasp of new knowledge and insight; at its worst it induces a regression to old answers and patterns of behaviour. The supervisor's interpretation is too much of a theory for John to digest yet, although a link has been made and seeds sown. John in his desperation shows that he is edging towards another kind of understanding. Perhaps the elderly tell their stories because 'that is all they have left to do'. The supervisor makes the most of this less threatening idea, and suggests that John read about the elderly in order to help him see things from their point of view.

## Phase 4: Experiment

There is no time left in their first meeting to consider what John will do with his next visit to the geriatric ward, and this omission has some ramifications as we shall see.

## Second meeting

The next meeting between John and his supervisor took place a week later, and John arrived late for it. Immediately he launched into an account of his success on the ward, and of how his learning from the previous meeting has begun to pay dividends. However, the cost of this emerges now in the relationship between him and his supervisor, whom he has kept waiting. The tension between them becomes the focus of the session, a new *experience* in itself. This will complicate the sequence we have been trying to keep in mind, by superimposing the *experience of supervision* upon that of the *work being supervised*. The whole session is taken over by the new experience. Confusing as this sounds we shall, nevertheless, see how the different levels of experience have an uncanny similarity. In fact, the relationship between the supervisor and the student begins to mirror the relationship between the student and his work.

J1:   Today was really good. I talked to this patient, or rather I listened to a really fascinating story of his childhood and experience in the war. I can see why old people need to talk, I could sense him enjoying himself more and more, piecing together bit by bit his life just as the book said. He kind of grew up before my eyes. I was there for ages, it was hard to come away.

S1:   That's quite a change from last week.

J2:   Yes, it certainly is.

S2:   Has it all been like that?

J3:   Well I am getting better at seeing who really wants to talk, and concentrating upon them. There is so much more point to that, than just trying to make conversation to some of the others. Some are very deaf and others just stare at you and don't want to know.

S3:   The ones who can't or won't tell their stories . . . ?

J4:   Mm . . . I suppose so.

S4:   What would it be like to spend time with them?

J5:   I don't know. I don't really see the point, particularly when there are people like Jim, who really genuinely need to talk, and have no one else to listen to them.

S5:   Your saying that reminds me of something you said last week, about your parents quarrelling over each other's parent, your grandparents. You can see some point in caring for Jim, but not for some of the others.

J6:   I don't know about that. I think ministry is about staying with the people that need you.

S6:   And shaking the dust off your feet of those who don't respond to you.

J7:   Well . . . yes.

S7:   And you, how do you feel when you are overlooked by a friend or colleague, who is busy with someone else?

J8:     I don't know . . . I think I would try to accept it, and not mind.

S8:     And how would you feel inside?

J9:     Well I expect I would feel a bit resentful.

S9:     I agree; that was how I was beginning to feel when you didn't turn up today. It's not a very acceptable feeling to have, and one that I would rather not own up to. And yet the feeling exists between us. You come in late and enthusiastic, and I am rather cool and apparently critical, and you begin to resent that.

J10:    Yes I did, I began to wonder what you wanted.

S10:    That you had done what I encouraged you to do last week, and I wasn't satisfied.

J11:    Yes a bit like that.

S11:    So we in a way were beginning to quarrel like your parents, to fight over who should and who should not be cared for.

J12:    That's amazing . . . you don't mean it's because of them?

S12:    Well what do you think?

J13:    I think that's rather far-fetched really.

S13:    Maybe it is, or maybe we are beginning to face some of the real difficulties of pastoral care. The conflict between what's satisfying and works, and what seems to make people angry, resentful and disillusioned.

J14:    I find it all very puzzling.

S14:    And upsetting, like you came in with the problem of pastoral care of the elderly well and truly beaten, and now you are not sure. So perhaps you can take your uncertainty with you to the placement. Keep going with Jim, but look around you as well. See who does get all the attention and who gets ignored, and see if you can see what the result of that is. I think you may find that your own experience from your family will actually help you be sensitive to what is going on, and the effect it has on the patients and staff.

## Experience and Reflection

As John tells his story it emerges that as well as beginning to see things from the point of view of the elderly—his new understanding from session one—he has also fallen back on previously learnt behaviour. He is dividing the elderly into those who need him and those who do not. His parents' method of managing their emotions was very similar. They felt love as well as responsibility towards their own parent and the opposite towards each other's. John has solved his problem of caring for the elderly by adopting his parents' solution. All would have been well for the time being, if he had not inadvertently upset his supervisor by being late for their meeting. This had the effect of bringing the ambivalence he had resolved within himself into his relationship with the supervisor. As is so often the case, actions and words are the bearers of different messages. John's words are positive, the experience he gives his supervisor, of which he is apparently unconscious, is negative. Unacceptable as his feelings are, the supervisor takes them seriously and relates them to his work with John and John's work with others. They are not to be disowned or condemned either in John or in himself. He begins to see how John will instinctively split his care, offering it to those who show they need him, and ignoring those who do not. He now has first hand *experience* of what it is like to be overlooked by John, and he shares that with him. The pity is that he then goes on too quickly to interpret it (phase 3) and convinces John, as the family battles did, that he, John, is somehow to blame. The supervision ends on a slightly more fruitful note with John's sense of confusion and questioning, and the supervisor's suggestion that John's family experience, rather than being to blame for anything, could in fact be an asset to him. It can help him be sensitive to the conflict and ambivalence in the work he is undertaking.

In their first two meetings the *experiences*, not from the work but from John's early life and the supervision, have dominated each occasion. Some reflection has been possible, but it has uncovered difficult and ambivalent feelings first within John and then between him and his supervisor. As we mentioned earlier there are always difficulties in trying to reflect on experience, particularly on those aspects which are painful and unacceptable. Students like John instinctively resist the kind of exploration which their experience pushes them towards, but for which they expect only criticism and judgement. They would like to know and understand phase 3 without the discomfort and uncertainty of phase 2. As we saw, it is all too easy for student and supervisor to move on to phase 3 prematurely when the anxiety of phase 2 is most acute. At the end of their second meeting, however, the supervisor helped John tolerate his anxiety sufficiently for him to be able to work with it, and to have it work for him in his placement. He did this by pointing out to John that the more sensitive he was to his own feelings the more aware he would be of those around him, and the more creative would be his ministry to them. Their third meeting shows how much John has begun to take in and use in his work. Initially he is unconscious of this, and is still preoccupied with his confusion and uncertainty. But as the session progresses we shall see how much more sensitive he has become to the atmosphere on his ward, and how he is able to make more of his observations. So much so that he moves quite naturally to a new understanding, phase 3, of those with whom he is working.

**Third meeting**

John arrives on time but his mood is thoughtful and withdrawn.

S1:  You look very thoughtful today?
J1:  Do I? I didn't realise that . . .
S2:  How would you describe your feelings?
J2:  (sighing) I don't know, a bit confused really . . . I'm not really sure what I'm meant to be doing.
S3:  What's expected?
J3:  What's expected . . . what do you mean?
S4:  Perhaps what I expect of you, when you come here, and when you go out visiting. Last week was difficult for us?
J4:  Yes I suppose it was. I remember feeling pleased with how last week went. Then when I came here you were cross because I was late, and seemed to be telling me I was ignoring people.

S5:   Yes that's what I mean, being confused about what you ought to be doing, and what I expect of you. I think you may have been quite angry with me when you left.

J5:   Yes I think I was.

S6:   And how do you feel now a week after?

J6:   Unsure and rather low . . .

S7:   And what effect has that had upon your work on the ward—with Jim and the others?

J7:   (*drawing himself together*) Well I did see Jim again, and that was good. He really seemed to appreciate my coming; but I did notice what you said; he gets a lot of attention. Some of the staff seem to be fighting over him at times, and others don't really get a look in. I'm sure that one of the patients on the women's side is really boiling up inside. She upsets everyone around her, but no one can get through to her.

S8:   Well imagine yourself as her for a moment. You are sitting in bed, is that what she does?

J8:   No, she's in a wheelchair usually, half blocking the way to the loos.

S9:   Well there you are then in your chair, and along I come as a chaplain to visit you; feeling a bit awkward I say, 'Hallo Mrs X how are you today?'. How would she reply?

J9:   (*with obvious pleasure assuming the part*) 'Miss X— typical of this place, no one knows who you are. Who are you anyway?'

S10:  'I'm sorry, I'm the chaplain just visiting.'

J10:  'Oh are you, and about time too. I've been asking to have my communion for weeks, and no one has bothered to come.'

S11:  'Oh I am sorry, shall I bring it for you tomorrow?'

J11:  'Not tomorrow, it's on Sunday that I want it, that's the Lord's day you know.'
      (*Both John and the supervisor dissolve into laughter.*)

S12:  She really is quite impossible isn't she?

J12:  Yes . . . Although I don't know, actually playing her was quite fun. I could see how stupid you looked, and how demeaning it felt to be visited by you. Like I expected you to patronise me, and I was going to get my retaliation in first.

S13: So maybe she's full of anger and resentment at her lot, and that's what she passes on to other people by her behaviour.

J13: Yes I think she does. She certainly makes everyone feel very resentful of her. One of the nurses was saying to me that she really ought to know better because she had been a missionary nurse herself.

S14: So she may think that too, that she ought to behave better, and because she can't or her resentment won't let her, she becomes even harder on herself and so harder on all of you.

J14: I think it is like that, but I can't work out why.

S15: Any more than she can?

J15: Right, it's not rational, and yet that's how it must be for her.

S16: You said that you enjoyed being her and giving me a hard time. Why do you think she might enjoy that.

J16: I don't know . . . (*his eyes suddenly lit up but then he appeared to dismiss the idea*).

S17: Yes, what was it you thought of just then.

J17: Well I don't see how it can be, but it was an enormous relief to be able to attack you, like it got something out of me that was a huge weight.

S18: I agree, I think you did, and I think you are right that she does need someone to take some of her burden, and hold it for a bit, and not return it with interest as usually happens.

J18: Yes, that's certainly true.

S19: I look forward to hearing more about her and about Jim, and I notice now that you are getting involved with the staff too and their care.

J19: What . . . what do you mean?

S20: Listening to the nurse's frustration about Miss X.

J20: Oh . . . I see.

It took John and his supervisor three meetings to begin to function effectively, and by measuring their work against this model we can see why. They had first to negotiate the resistance that this learning always provokes. Learners will feel that their experience, or more often their lack of it, will condemn them, and that the expert supervisor will belittle their efforts and suggest that they take up some other work. So inhibited can they be by such fears that they either avoid experience as much as possible and talk as John did in generalities, or else they are so defensive and selective in their reflections that they limit themselves to seeing only that which will call forth old patterns and solutions. This resistance to learning has first to be confronted and students helped to manage their anxiety sufficiently to give themselves a chance to learn. This happened for John and allowed him to move from the extreme positions of general failure and selective success to a more uneasy but also a more sensitive position. From there he could begin to expand his understanding, grasp new ideas, and want more adequate and less partial solutions. He had begun to see that all behaviour can be understood, and that in striving to understand, the carer is enabled to engage with, but not be overcome by, the emotional and irrational pressures from within and from without.

### Fourth meeting

This is illustrated in the next meeting with the supervisor, when John comes ready to talk about his visits to Miss X. The previous week's discussion has had an effect upon the way he approached her and this has borne some fruit. He wants now to make some sense of his thoughts and reflections, and he presents these without any prompting.

J1:   I would like to talk about Miss X today. I'm not sure what to do next.

S1:   All right, tell me what's been happening since we met.

J2:   Well, I've made a point of spending time with her. At first, of course, she was very cool and unwelcoming, but then she began trying to provoke me, I think. She asked about my training, or rather told me about it, and said how much the Church's standards had slipped. She pointed out that when she trained, things were done properly. So I asked her to tell me about it. That wasn't a very good move, as she said she hadn't time to go on talking to me and promptly shut her eyes. I asked her if I could come back and hear about it another time, but she didn't reply. So after a bit I got up and left.

S2: That sounds as though you got some way with her.
J3: Does it? I wasn't sure.
S3: Not sure of what?
J4: I felt as though I'd gone too far. Kind of intruding on her, and she didn't want that, or something like it.
S4: Good. I think that sounds quite likely. And you gave her time and also space to decide for herself.
J5: Yes, that's true.
S5: How could you test out your uncertainty?
J6: I could ask her again if she wanted to tell me. Or make it easier for her to say she was tired.
S6: Being direct or indirect with her?
J7: Direct I think. She is with me.
S7: So how would you put it to her, what will you say?
J8: Oh heavens . . . 'I've come again to bother you, and hear about when you were training. But only if you feel like telling me.' How does that sound?
S8: How does it sound to you?
J9: Not so good really.
S9: I think it could sound a bit abrupt to her. She didn't like you questioning her, and she preferred to speak for you as well. I liked the way you did it last time letting her take the lead. In that way you leave the decision to her. She knows you are interested now.
J10: Mm . . . I see what you mean.
There's another thing I have been wondering about and that is her aggressiveness. All the nurses are fed up with her now. They say how bad nurses are at being patients, and, for my benefit I think, that Christian ones are the worst! And in her case it's true. She really is very bitter.
S10: What would make you feel bitter like that?
J11: I don't know . . . If I was badly let down, and by someone close to me. I think I could be very hurt and resentful then. But only to the person who let me down, not to everyone else.
S11: And if you couldn't get at the one who let you down what then?
J12: Mm . . . I would have to take it out on someone in the end.

S12: And she has no visitors, she's driven everyone away?

J13: That's right, she has no one to attack but us.

S13: She sounds very hurt to me, somehow like Job, but not close enough to God to be able to take it out on him.

J14: Perhaps it is God who has let her down. And after all the things she has done for him, a nurse and a missionary!

S14: You may well be right about that. I wonder if she came across Job or Jeremiah in her training?

J15: (*smiling*) Mm . . . I wonder.

This fourth meeting marks the completion of the phases of the learning sequence for John. The order has not been as precise as the ideal suggests, but nevertheless he has been able to *anticipate and rehearse* (phase 4) how he will next engage with Miss X, and this has developed out of his *experience* with her (phase 1), his *reflections and thoughts* about that (phase 2), and the *understanding* of her that he reached in this meeting (phase 3). He takes up the supervisor's suggestion of continuing his present strategy with her: letting her take the lead while showing that he is not put off by her. In the meantime he also tries to extend his *understanding* of her aggressiveness (phase 3), and the supervisor encourages him to *imagine himself* (phase 2) in her position. He feels let down and hurt; and being unable to take his revenge on the one who let him down he attacks others indiscriminately. This in turn reminds the supervisor of Job: let down by God, angry and bitter at his lot. So the suffering of Job becomes a potential resource for both student and patient (phase 3).

Experience and practice rarely fit neatly with the theories which are derived from them, and this is no exception. Throughout the four meetings which we have studied, John and the supervisor have moved through each of the phases, not always in the prescribed order, but sufficiently for us to see the importance of each phase, how it prepares the ground for the next one, and so contributes to the process of learning from experience. At the same time we have seen how learning is distorted and practice undermined when a phase is ignored or over-emphasised.

## Notes

1. Kolb, D. A., Rubin, I. M., and McIntyre, J. M., *Organisational Psychology; an Experiential Approach*, New Jersey: Prentice-Hall 1974. See also Thomas, D. L., 'A Theory of Education Relevant to CPE', *Journal for Supervision and Training for Ministry*, vol. 5 1982.
2. Blythe, R., *The View in Winter*, Penguin 1979.

# FOUR

# Learning and Authority

_____

In the last chapter we concentrated upon the central relationship of supervision as the medium through which learning takes place. In as far as student and supervisor can employ the phases of the sequence we outlined, experience will foster learning, and theory and practice will complement one another. The educational goal is, however, only one part of the overall objective of supervision. In the case of John and his placement, for instance, as well as his relationship with his supervisor, there were a number of other significant figures and institutions which impinged on their work together.

Foremost amongst these were the two patients Jim and Miss X to whom John ministered, the hospital where John had been placed, the college which required him to have this training, and of course the shadowy but no less significant figures of his parents and grandparents. John's learning was taking place within the context of his ministry to others. It was influenced by his own life experience and was under the scrutiny of his ecclesiastical authorities, who had to decide upon his fitness for this work. This illustrates that there are management and administrative goals to supervision as well as educational ones, and that it is likely that John the learner and John the future minister will expect rather different things from the whole process. Whereas the former will look for help, encouragement and greater understanding, the latter may fear criticism, judgement and even condemnation. The educational and administrative objectives of supervision can, and often will, pull the work in different and sometimes opposing directions.

In their classic work on the teaching and learning of psychotherapy, Ekstein and Wallerstein identified this tension as central to the work of supervision, being the essential ingredient in the training and development of effective professionals.[1] They represented this diagrammatically in what they called the Clinical Rhombus:

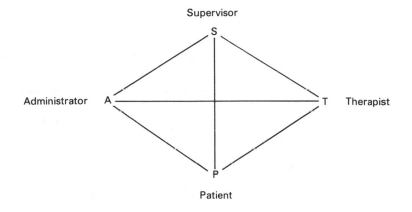

The training of therapists and the oversight of their work is the responsibility of their supervisors, who need to keep in mind all the figures in the Rhombus and their relationship to one another. The relationships between the Patient and the Therapist P—T and the Therapist and the Supervisor T—S are obviously important. But supervisors as the qualified professionals and representatives of the agency or institution have a responsibility for the welfare of the agency's patient or client. The student's learning must not be at the expense of the patient's treatment. Although it is often difficult to judge this, supervisors have a responsibility to intervene on the patient's behalf if in their opinion there is any conflict of interest, hence the line across the centre of the Rhombus S—P. The fourth corner is entitled Administrator, to represent the institution within which the therapy is taught and practised. The clinic or hospital which appoints the Supervisor A—S, offers a service to the Patient A—P, and training to the Therapist A—T. The institution through the Administrator would require different things of all the others. The Supervisor is to promote the philosophy and methods of the clinic and to ensure that its standards are maintained, the Therapist is to learn and to practise effectively, while the Patient benefits from, and pays for, the service given. In turn the others will expect the institution to provide them with the necessary resources to meet these responsibilities. Complicated as this is, the authors see in this constellation rich opportunities for the training and development of therapists. In their book they show how the corners of the Rhombus represent not only the significant external figures, but also the important internal pressures and influences within a student's own mind.

As the student in his corner faces the other three corners of his clinical world, he confronts three kinds of problems which, we hope to demonstrate, are but the external representations of typical inner situations. He is to help the patient and has to acquire skills in order to cope with the seeming chaos that to him the illness of the patient represents. To the supervisor he brings his own chaos, his own difficulties and lack of knowledge and skill, in order to be helped toward increasing mastery and growing competence. And finally, the administrator represents chiefly the conditions and requirements of the clinical situation that the student has to meet, and the approval or disapproval of the work that he is doing. As he goes on with the task of acquiring psychotherapeutic skills, he has to face these same aspects of himself. He has to cope with the anarchic, unorganised aspects of his professional self; he has to develop skills, and grow in technical and human competence; and he has to struggle with the task of having to live by regulations and living up to professional ideals. This is illustrated by the diagram below:

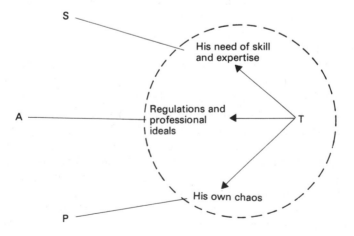

Returning to John, it is clear that in his work he was confronted by some internal reflections of the people he encountered. These can be represented by the figure of the Rhombus. When he came to his first meeting he was ambivalent about his experience: he 'supposed' it was all right. But when he was questioned further he admitted to the 'demanding' effect of the patients, their telling of the same story over and over again. The John/patient relationship comes into focus and is immediately explored from John's point of view from within his mind:

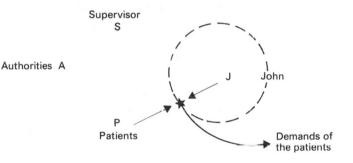

He looks for help to resolve the tension he feels, an authority to support him. Although he does not like it, he has to behave with kindness. 'It's just the way I've been brought up'. In John's mind it is his parents and their authority which face him across the Rhombus:

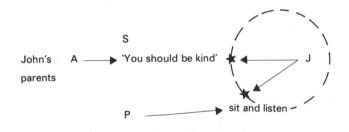

The supervisor helps John explore the nature of that authority and together they uncover the mixed messages which his parents gave: be kind to some and resent others.

John has received this message and now operates with this authority in mind. 'Some of the patients are super, but others just witter on without any reason to what they say.' The supervisor's suggestion that it is difficult for John to tolerate them or to see why they do it, conveys sufficient acceptance of John's feelings for him to be able to look beyond his parents and grandparents — the elderly in his mind — towards the ones he is meeting on the ward. He is free to think about why they talk as they do: 'I suppose that's all they've got left to do'. The supervisor then suggests that John extend his understanding by drawing on another authority. 'Why don't you have a look at what Ronald Blythe has written. *The View in Winter* has a lot about old people and their stories':

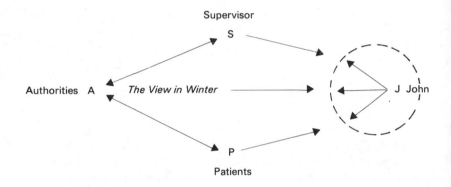

Ekstein and Wallerstein go on to show how supervision provides the necessary arena in which both external and internal actors are acknowledged and respected, and in which students are enabled to develop their professional identity and competence from both within and without.

We will now explore this model in relation to the pastoral supervision offered by a vicar to his curate during the first year of the latter's ministry. The following is an account of the curate's work with a parishioner called Evelyn. She had been confined to her home and to a wheelchair for some years as she suffered from multiple sclerosis. A week after the curate's first visit to her, she was found dead by the home help. The vicar and curate meet to talk about it on the day after the funeral. The vicar begins by asking Nigel, the curate, to tell him what happened and his reactions to it. Nigel recounted how he received a telephone message about Evelyn's death. He immediately went to see her neighbour, and with the help of the Social Services department managed to trace Evelyn's brother, the next of kin, and persuaded him to have the funeral in their church. The vicar then asked Nigel how he had reacted to these events. Their conversation went like this (C = Curate, V = Vicar):

C1: I was still slightly bewildered by the fact of her death, I think everybody was. She didn't look to be about to die when I saw her. People were worried. What if she had taken her own life? The neighbour mentioned it, and then said it couldn't be the case.

V1: And what did you think?

C2: I didn't know and told her there was no point in speculating as the post mortem would tell us what had happened. She had this place in a sheltered home, therefore it seemed unlikely.

V2: Nevertheless it crossed your mind just as it had her neighbour's. It was a difficult thought to hang on to?

C3: Mmm . . . I didn't think it was really likely.

V3: Maybe that wasn't the point, more that you both could imagine someone in Evelyn's position considering suicide as a way out.

C4: Yes I see what you mean. It would only be natural to consider it.

V4: Did you have any other reactions?

C5: I was a bit sad . . . and, yes, I felt slightly guilty in a funny way because I had seen her. That she had slipped through the net of the people who had been supposed to care.

V5: Did that sense of guilt last?

C6: No, I told myself that it was irrational.

V6: And did that work?

C7: What do you mean?

V7: Can you rid yourself of feelings by telling yourself they are irrational?

C8: Oh I see. Yes, usually I can.

As the supervision begins we can see something of the relationships involved and how these are reflected in the Rhombus:

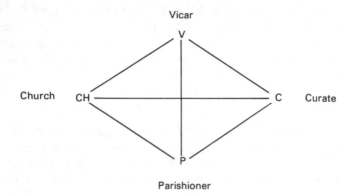

Nigel in his work with Evelyn [C−P] has been confronted first with a degenerative illness which cannot be cured, and then, in less than a week, with the death of his parishioner. There could be few more daunting experiences for an embryo pastor to have to face. Nigel is at once exposed to some of the most chaotic and irrational elements of pastoral work. His response is naturally to try and protect himself from that chaos by being as rational as possible. To do this he has to discount his thoughts about suicide as pointless, and repress his feeling of guilt as irrational. In protecting himself from both the inner and the outer pressures of the C−P relationship, he has in effect cut himself off from the learning that the C−V relationship could offer him. Thinking and feeling make him so vulnerable that he cannot afford to do either. He hopes that the post mortem will relieve him of these anxieties. Recognising this the vicar sets out to help him manage a little more thought. He invites Nigel to imagine himself in Evelyn's position, and from there to see how natural it was to consider suicide, and therefore how appropriate it might be for him to have thought of it. The vicar is less successful in helping Nigel keep a grip on his feeling of guilt, probably because he could identify with it himself and wanted some protection too. Nigel's technique is to make it irrational and then to dismiss it altogether. The vicar cannot contain his surprise and envy. If we follow the progress of their meeting a little further we can see what happens to the feeling of guilt.

V8:  Perhaps if you hadn't contacted the social worker you would have felt more guilty.

C9:  I tried to think back to see if there was anything that I hadn't noticed. There was just the MS, but then I'm not a doctor.

V9:  What more might have been done for Evelyn?

C10:  I don't know to be honest. I'm not convinced that a lot of people visiting her would have made any difference. It appears that a lot of people cared, the Social Services and us, and still she can contract a nasty illness and die. It seems totally ridiculous!

V10:  Thinking back to our last meeting was there not a lot of neglect, so that all the supposed help did not add up to much. Whose fault, if any, was that?

C11:  Must be the fault of the professionals, not of the friendly droppers-in.

V11:  Why is that?

C12:  Because a professional is paid to do a job. Volunteers may spend more time, but professionals have the power. They put in that ridiculous heater she couldn't operate. I don't blame the workmen, some of them thought it was a good idea. They should feel a bit guilty.

The vicar encourages Nigel to explore the feeling of guilt further. He tries but he cannot trace it very far either within himself or within the context of the pastoral care given to Evelyn by the congregation [P—CH]. Everyone did what they could and she still got ill and died. This avenue takes Nigel straight back to the irrational and chaotic nature of illness and death, in the face of which ordinary people can do nothing. It is 'totally ridiculous'. The vicar is not so easily distracted from the search for the guilt's true home. He recalls their last discussion about all the neglect that Evelyn suffered, and he presses Nigel to identify who is to blame for this. Incidentally this also saves him from having to face the total ridiculousness of sudden illness and death. Nigel is only too pleased to make his escape too. He puts the blame firmly on the 'professionals', who have power, knowledge and expertise. He had, of course, dissociated himself from them early on by saying he was no doctor. The guilt and the blame come to rest with the agencies who exist to cure illness and prevent death. For the moment they appear in Nigel's mind in the left hand corner of the Rhombus replacing the church (which through the congregation did all that it could), and allow him to avoid his own sense of inadequacy as a 'professional' by identifying professionalism, and failed professionalism at that, with social work and medicine. The vicar misses this opportunity to help Nigel see what he is doing, probably because he too is wondering how to manage his sense of failure. Guilt and blame are notoriously difficult to address and are almost inevitably projected away towards authorities and organisations who are not immediately represented and are conveniently fallible. This sequence demonstrates how important the figure of the Rhombus is. It represents the psychological boundaries within which projections need to be contained, so that they can be understood and learnt from. If projections are allowed to break out of those boundaries and come to rest on absent objects and individuals, then they will be out of reach of student and supervisor. So Nigel lost an important opportunity to build up his professional identity as a pastor able to confront feelings of guilt, failure and even blame. At the same time he got away with stereotyping other professionals as bad and uncaring, making it that much more difficult for himself to learn to be more professional.

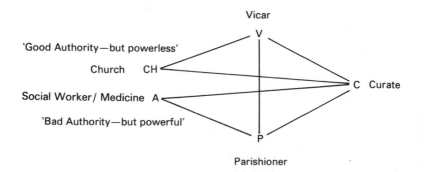

Parishioner

The vicar of course is not responsible to either the social services or to the medical establishment as he is to the church. This allows Nigel to split the authority corner of the Rhombus and project failure and incompetence onto the professional agencies, leaving the church, including himself and the vicar, relatively unscathed.

The supervision continued with some discussion about the funeral:

V12: How was the funeral for you?
C13: I found it rather sad. There was failure in the air, corporate not individual. The family were sitting apart: they looked awkward and unhappy. It was good to see so many from the congregation there, but then you asked them to come and they always do if you ask.
V13: We needed them didn't we?
C14: Yes we did. It was the best thing about it. Having Evelyn there for the last time surrounded by people who in their own way did care about her, or tried to.
V14: And who were sad and guilty because they, we, hadn't done all that we would have liked to have done.
C15: Yes I was glad you mentioned that at the service.
V15: There's a need for confession, an acknowledgement of our humanity and mortality. Funerals bring that home more than anything else does, I think.

Nigel and the vicar explore the way in which their organisation, the church, helped them to grieve for Evelyn and face the effect her death had had upon them. The service had contained the variety of feelings and thoughts which emerged earlier and were more or less avoided. There they had been able to admit their sense of failure and guilt, and to put it more in proportion with their humanity and mortality. Sufficient order had been created out of the chaos for family and friends to let go of Evelyn, and to bear with their feelings about her and themselves. The church in the form of the congregation had come to the aid of the professional pastors, making the Rhombus intact again, by supporting and containing all the actors in this drama and their relationships with one another:

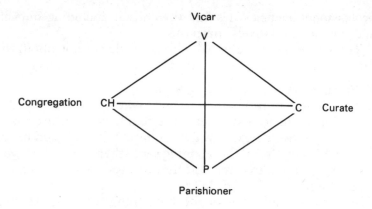

## Note

1. Ekstein, R., and Wallerstein, R. S., *The Teaching and Learning of Psychotherapy*, 2nd edn, New York: International Universities Press, 1972 p. 11.

FIVE

# Learning and Theology

The characteristic of pastoral supervision which sets it apart from all other types of supervision is its theological perspective. The approach to supervision outlined up to now is heavily dependent upon methods developed in other caring professions. It could not be otherwise, for both pastoral care and its related educational structures involve human relationships, sometimes of a complex nature. Pastoral relationships are first and foremost human relationships with all the dynamics of such relationships.

Yet pastoral relationships must also be viewed from another perspective, a perspective which is best described by the word 'theological'. The theological nature of such relationships may however be subject to as many interpretations, both explicit and implicit, as there are interpreters.

The person offering pastoral care inevitably brings to the task a certain theological perspective. For an ordained minister this will be rooted in an academic theological education and a personal experience of the life of the Church; for a divinity student it will be part of a developing viewpoint still being worked out in the formative years of professional education; and a lay person, while perhaps claiming to be ignorant of the theological niceties, may bring a deep implicit faith growing out of a lifetime's participation in the worship and witness of the Church.

Theological issues may also be important for the person on the receiving end of pastoral care, though these may not be as sharply defined as for the carer. Sometimes they may loom large in the conscious mind. Is this minister going to try and convert me? Or ask me to go to church? Or tell me I'm a sinner? And sometimes unconscious factors are at work, whose origins lie deep within previous and forgotten encounters, both positive and negative, with ministers and priests, and with God. For the supervisor especially, theological questions cannot be avoided, precisely because central to pastoral supervision is the need to enable the person who is offering care under supervision to integrate theological understanding with pastoral practice.

In this chapter we will turn again to case material in order to describe the supervision of Rachel, a theological student undertaking a placement in a psychiatric hospital. Inevitably some of the themes already discussed will recur, but in the case of Rachel we will pay special attention to the way in which the insights gained in the placement relate to her developing theological understanding. In order to do this, it is necessary to explore theoretically some of the ways of relating theological insights to the practice of pastoral care.

The theology of pastoral care has been dominated, at least until recently, by two very different approaches to the relationship between theology and practice. The first begins with theological principles and seeks to apply them to the practice of ministry; we shall call this the 'Applied Theology' model. The starting point for the second model is to be found in a secular understanding of human relationships and accords an altogether different status to theological concepts; this may be described as an 'Applied Psychology' model. Each of these will be examined in some detail. It will be argued that neither provides a satisfactory basis for the integration of theology and practice in pastoral education. A third approach will then be proposed which draws on what has come to be known as 'Narrative Theology.'

## Pastoral Care as Applied Theology

> Like the proclamation of the church generally, pastoral conversation has as its only content the communication of the forgiveness of sins in Jesus Christ . . . man in his totality is addressed as a sinner under grace.[1]

Thus Eduard Thurneysen encapsulates an understanding of the theology of pastoral care which has had a dominant influence in Europe for the greater part of this century. Pastoral care is a form of proclamation, where the Word is addressed to the individual rather than to the congregation.

Although the form in which the Word is communicated may have to be adapted to accommodate the needs of the individual, it is nevertheless the content, rather than the form, of the proclamation which is of primary importance. In this model the locus of theological learning is the classroom, the library and the Bible study group. It is in these settings that theological concepts are assimilated, and it is in the placement that the learner attempts to apply these concepts. Important repercussions for pastoral education ensue and are described by J. D. and E. E. Whitehead as follows:

> The student can easily come to understand his role as that of applying what theologians have reflected upon and decided. His ministry does not include his own theologizing, but rather his application of someone else's theologizing to his own specific ministerial situation.[2]

The task of supervision then becomes that of discovering how appropriately the learner has applied theological concepts to specific pastoral situations. In this model of pastoral care, sometimes referred to as the 'proclamatory' model, the relationship between theological and psychological views of man was very clearly defined. Psychological perspectives had their own integrity but they made no contribution to a theological understanding. 'We shall really understand man only when we understand him from the Bible.'[3] In Europe pastoral theology and the secular therapies developed in virtual isolation from one another. Theology could only be applied to the concrete situation and the role of the theological educator was to enable the learner to do just that.

### Pastoral Care as Applied Psychology

If the previous model of pastoral care was concerned with the application of abstract theological ideas to concrete pastoral situations, the approach to which we now turn has as its focus the acquisition of ministerial skills. While the first approach was described as a proclamatory model, that presently under consideration may appropriately be categorised as a 'therapeutic' model. Here the focus is not on proclamation but on the nature of the pastoral relationship; and if the first approach has its roots in European neo-orthodoxy, the origins of the therapeutic model of pastoral care are mainly North American.

Quotations from two Americans who have had a formative influence on the development of pastoral counselling in their own country (and beyond) illustrate this approach which is based on very different presuppositions. Thus Hiltner, while maintaining that the basic aim of pastoral counselling is the same as that of the Church itself—to bring people to Christ and the Christian fellowship—has a very wide conception of the nature of the enterprise:

> Broadly speaking the special aim of pastoral counselling may be stated as the attempt by a pastor to help people help themselves through the process of gaining understanding of their inner conflicts.[4]

For Carroll Wise, the goal of counselling is insight:

> The capacity of the human mind to see into and understand itself and its motives once it is placed in an understanding relationship is one of the gifts of grace to mankind.[5]

It is only towards the end of their respective books that Hiltner and Wise attempt to relate counselling practice to the Christian faith, the former listing the 'religious resources' which may be drawn upon to facilitate the process of personal growth, the latter seeing these resources as being communicated through the person rather than through the words of the pastor.

This understanding of pastoral care was highly influential during the formative years of the development of clinical pastoral education and pastoral counselling in North America. The emphasis was on growth in self-awareness, interpersonal skills and counselling techniques. It was an understandable reaction against an approach to ministry which lacked a coherent theory of the person, but its consequences were not uniformly beneficial. The positive gains were that pastoral care learned much from secular therapists such as Carl Rogers,[6] and that personality theories and counselling skills were seen to be relevant for ministry. The unhappy consequence was that all too often the theological dimension of ministry was lost, together with the social and political dimensions. The focus of supervision became the acquisition of skills, often of a purely secular nature (excellent in themselves), rather than the formation of pastoral identity. A frequent outcome was that a student attained a high degree of proficiency in these skills and left the ministry to use them in some secular profession. While theological learning of a personal nature is absent from the 'Applied Theology' model, because it involves no more than the application of a second-hand theology, it is lacking in the 'Applied Psychology' model because theological issues are never addressed.

At the end of the day both the proclamatory model and the therapeutic model lead to the separation of theology and practice. A reason for this may lie in a failure to examine the assumptions behind the whole exercise of theological integration. If it is assumed, even implicitly, that theological integration is no more than a matter of seeking to make tidy connections between theological concepts and the practice of ministry, then the attempt to relate theology and practice remains an intellectual exercise with the attendant splitting already noted. But supposing we are talking about a process which has an altogether deeper and more personal dimension in the life of the learner. Then the process of integration would take on a very different character involving not only ideas gleaned from books (a learned theology), but also the most basic beliefs and values of the learner, growing out of a total life experience (an owned theology). Then integration would be truly seen as a process to be initiated and not simply as some goal to be reached. Perhaps Niebuhr's phrase 'the relevance of an impossible ideal'[7] is apt here, because in reality the integration issue is never resolved for any of us. To reflect theologically on the practice of ministry is to be engaged in a cyclical process of integration, disintegration, under pressure from the realities of ministry or of fresh theological insights, and subsequent reintegration. The task of supervision then becomes one of enabling learners to begin a process which will continue throughout their ministry. We turn therefore to another way of relating theology and practice, which though more complex provides a more satisfactory framework for the kind of theological integration which is central to pastoral education.

### Theological Integration through the Interaction of Stories

In this approach it is assumed that theological reflection upon the practice of ministry draws on material from three sources: (a) the historic beliefs of the community of faith contained in Scripture and the theological tradition; (b) the realities of the pastoral situation; and (c) the life experience of the one who offers care. In this model the process of theological reflection is essentially trialogical, with three sources being allowed to interact with one another.

A consideration of the nature of these three sources will reveal that each has a narrative quality, and can be expressed in story form. Thus to speak of the historic beliefs of the community of faith is to be in touch with a religious tradition which is deeply rooted in stories: stories of the people of God in the Old Testament; the life of Jesus Christ, who himself used story as a major vehicle of his teaching; the life of the early Church to which the New Testament bears witness; and the Church as it has developed down through the ages. The Christian tradition has at its centre, not abstract theological concepts, but stories of people and events. Thus in the story of the encounter with the risen Christ on the road to Emmaus[8] we see examples of different types of biblical narrative. There is a reference to Messianic expectation in the Old Testament ('We had hoped he was the one to redeem Israel'); there is a recounting of the story of Jesus—his life and the events surrounding his death; and there is the interpretation of the story by Christ himself ('beginning with Moses . . .')

Further, there can be few pastoral situations encountered which do not involve a human story. Indeed most pastoral conversations will begin by inviting someone (perhaps not in so many words) to tell his or her story, or that part of it which seems to be of immediate concern. Of course the story told will not be a simple recounting of 'the facts'—what story is?—but will embody the storyteller's understanding of the facts. Sometimes, perhaps always, the task of pastoral care is to enable someone to reinterpret his or her own life story.

Finally in pastoral care there is always another story to be considered and that is the story of the carer. Those who become involved in caring for others bring to their ministry all their previous experience of life. This experience together with the values, motives, prejudices and 'hang-ups' constitute the story of the carer's life and make their impact upon any ministry offered. When Jesus identified Nathaniel as 'an Israelite in whom there is no guile', he was obviously drawing upon some past experience!

The contribution of narrative theology to pastoral care has been developed in recent American writing. In *The Living Human Document: Re-visioning Pastoral Counseling in a Hermeneutical Mode* Charles Gerkin writes:

> The Pastoral Counselor as a Bearer of Stories
>
> The pastoral counselor is not only a listener to stories; he or she is also a bearer of stories and a story. The pastoral counselor does not come empty-handed to the task of understanding the other's story and offering the possibility of a new interpretation. The pastoral counselor brings his or her own interpretation of life experience with its use of both commonly held symbols, images and themes from the cultural milieu of the counselor, and the private, nuanced meanings that have been shaped by the pastoral counselor's own life experience and its private interpretation.[9]

Gerkin is drawing upon the imagery of Anton Boisen, the 'father' of Clinical Pastoral Education in the United States, who stated that there was no better library for the study of pastoral theology than the 'living human documents'[10] of people in crisis. Boisen maintained that the language and life experience of someone grappling with deep personal issues had to be interpreted in much the same way as a biblical text. To interpret the human documents pastoral counsellors may employ a number of secular therapies. But their work must be firmly grounded in the Christian faith.

The word 'hermeneutics' generally refers to the theory of the interpretation of written texts. This begins by determining the original meaning of the text and leads to its elucidation for modern readers. Similarly in pastoral counselling, the understanding of a human life is seen essentially as a hermeneutical task. The pastoral counsellor seeks to understand the story of another person's life, not only for the significance of what happened at some time in the past, but also what this may mean at the present time. This involves both counsellor and client in establishing communication across the boundaries of a language and life situation which may both unite and divide them.

This theme is also expounded by Donald Capps in his book *Pastoral Care and Hermeneutics.*[11] Drawing upon the work of Paul Ricoeur, Capps sets out the view that since texts and meaningful human actions are sufficiently similar, methods and theories developed for interpreting texts may also be used for interpreting human actions. Thus Capps postulates a hermeneutical model for pastoral care, demonstrating that such a model can be helpful for understanding what a given pastoral situation means to each of the persons involved.

In pastoral supervision, the theological task is to facilitate both the interpretation of stories and their mutual interaction, enabling the learner to understand not only the story of the person receiving pastoral care in the light of the story at the centre of the faith, but also the relationship between these stories and his or her own story.

A contemporary exponent of narrative theology, G. W. Stroup, uses a stronger word than 'interaction' when he writes of the importance of stories in the development of fundamental theological understanding:

> Revelation becomes an experienced reality at that juncture where the narrative identity of an individual collides with the narrative identity of the Christian community.[12]

Perhaps we could go a stage further and postulate that theological integration becomes an experienced reality in supervision at that juncture where the narrative identity of the pastor collides both with the narrative identity of the Christian community and with the narrative quality of the pastoral situation.

It might be questioned whether 'collision' with its overtones of destructive energy is the best metaphor to describe the process of theological integration. Perhaps the imagery of sexual intercourse captures more accurately the reality of what happens. For intercourse implies a sensitivity in meeting with both partners giving and receiving, so that something new is brought to birth in a relationship which is mutually satisfying.

## Theological Reflection as a three-way process

Reference has twice been made to the work of the Whiteheads in criticising what were considered to be inadequate models for theological reflection in pastoral care. In the paper referred to, published in 1975, outlining three models of field education, they questioned field education both as the application of theology and as the acquisition and development of ministerial skills. They then proposed a third model which at that time they considered a more satisfactory alternative, namely, 'Field Education as the Locus of Pastoral Theology'. In this model theological insight and pastoral experience were allowed to interact.

The theological reflection in this model is two-directional: the student learns how to allow his experience to question his theological tradition as well as how to allow the tradition to confront his experience.[13]

In a later and more substantial work they develop this two-dimensional model into the kind of three-dimensional model described above, which they set out schematically as follows:[14]

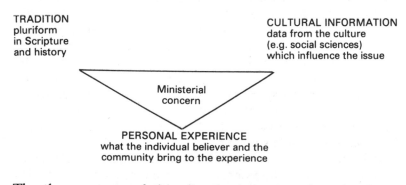

TRADITION
pluriform
in Scripture
and history

CULTURAL INFORMATION
data from the culture
(e.g. social sciences)
which influence the issue

Ministerial
concern

PERSONAL EXPERIENCE
what the individual believer and the
community bring to the experience

The three corners of this diagram correspond to the three sources of theological reflection outlined above. TRADITION corresponds to the stories from Scripture and the Christian tradition, CULTURAL INFORMATION to the human story central to the pastoral situation, which may be illuminated by the human sciences, and PERSONAL EXPERIENCE to the life story of the carer.

Having identified this three-fold source of theological reflection, the Whiteheads then propose a three-stage method by which these three sources may interact. The three stages are *Attending, Assertion* and *Decision-making.*

In *attending,* the essential tasks of the carer are to listen and learn: to listen creatively to the realities of the pastoral situation by listening to the story; to hear what the human sciences have to say about it by listening, for instance, to the deepest emotions of a bereaved person or by hearing what psychologists and sociologists have to teach about bereavement; to listen to what Scripture says about death and eternal life; and to learn from the ways in which the Church has in the past cared for the bereaved; to listen to, and be in touch with, one's own feelings about death and important experiences of personal loss, and to learn what this past experience teaches about our reactions to such situations. This kind of listening is active rather than passive. It involves a suspension of premature judgements and a holding back until all that can be heard has been heard.

In the second stage, that of *assertion,* these three sources are allowed to interact, facilitating what Stroup refers to as the 'collision of narratives', permitting the religious tradition *and* the raw data of the situation *and* personal feelings and experience to have their due place in the reflection process; and preventing any one of them from either dominating or being neglected. It might again be questioned whether the word 'assertion' describes exactly what is going on here. Like 'collision' it has an aggressive overtone which is foreign to the process. Again the idea of interpenetration captures more precisely the mutual relationship which is in operation between these three sources.

It is on the basis of attending and assertion that *decision-making* can proceed, as proceed it must amidst the realities of life. At this point the Whiteheads point out the crucial difference between *theological decisions* and *ministerial decisions*:

The minister reflects in order to act. In the face of insufficient information or conflicting facts, a reflection accountable only to the criteria of academic theology can decide not to decide. Instead the theologian can appropriately reinitiate the process of reflection in the hope of coming to greater clarity sometime in the future. A ministerial reflection most generally focusses on a question that demands practical resolution now. In many cases the minister or the community must act even in the face of insufficient information.[16]

Thus the whole process of theological reflection is directed towards a pastoral practice that takes seriously not only the realities of the human situation but also the insights of the theological tradition and the personal experience of the carer. It does not guarantee that right decisions will always be taken, only that action will be well-informed and therefore potentially more accurate more often. It contributes to a pastoral care which can be effective in the face of inherent ambiguities because these ambiguities, having been explored in the light of all the available information, can be lived with. Yet we do not have to be right all the time. In his *Ethics*, Bonhoeffer makes the helpful distinction between the 'ultimate' and the 'penultimate'.[17] To the sphere of the penultimate belongs all human action whether that action be an ethical commitment, or the consequences of a ministerial decision. The final word, the word of salvation, belongs to the realm of the ultimate, to God himself. For the Christian there is always the possibility of repentance and forgiveness. In Nicholas Montserrat's novel, *The Cruel Sea*, the commander of a destroyer is confronted with an impossible choice between two courses of action each of which will have tragic consequences. His tormented cry is, 'One must do what one must do—and say one's prayers'. If this is an eloquent summary of that ethical dilemma, it can also be the only response to certain ministerial decisions. We are justified not by our works, but by the grace of God's forgiveness.

In the light of this somewhat theoretical discussion we shall now see how these concepts may be of some practical relevance in the supervision of one particular student.

## RACHEL'S STORY

So we turn to the story of Rachel, a theological student who undertook a placement in a psychiatric hospital. While we will be concerned with all the dimensions of the supervision process, we will be particularly interested to see how Rachel is helped to handle those theological issues which are invariably present when care is offered bearing the label 'pastoral'.

### Expectations

Setting up a placement can be a complex business. As we shall see in chapter 9, one reason for this is that all the parties involved approach it with their own expectations regarding objectives and outcome. The student comes both with high hopes about its potential contribution to her preparation for ministry and deep fears about the possible risks of encountering the unknown. Rachel had her own special reasons for wanting a placement in a psychiatric hospital as she described:

Many years ago I watched a film on television called *The Snake Pit*. In the USA of fifty years ago, a woman was admitted to a big state mental hospital where she encountered a nightmare world of unsympathetic, goading staff, deluded manipulative fellow-patients and appalling prison-like conditions. She came to see herself as trapped in a pit of snakes and from that moment on she strove to get out and ultimately succeeded.

This film made a great impression on me. The image of psychiatry that it presented was, of course, dated, but its portrayal of the sick woman was painfully convincing. In my family one of my great aunts had spent fifteen years in a mental hospital. As a trainee minister I realised that this might be an area of ministry I should explore so I applied to work at a psychiatric hospital for my pastoral placement.

My starting point was thus a particular sympathy for the psychiatrically ill, and an interest in psychiatric medicine and therapy. I also possessed a conviction that the alienation that mental illness so often brings about between the sufferer and his family and friends, does not take place between the sufferer and God; that God must love and be with those in mental darkness as with those in health. In preparation for the placement I read two books on psychiatry, two on chaplaincy and two novels related to this theme. I also made regular visits under the chaplain's auspices to two wards of a local psychiatric hospital, and spent one very full and valuable day with the chaplain. All these preparations gave some preliminary insight and knowledge on which to found my response to what I would encounter.

Thus Rachel brought to the placement certain matters arising from her own life story: memories of a film about a psychiatric hospital which had made a deep impression upon her, and the fact that a member of her family had spent a large part of her life in such an institution. She also realised that this was an area which might be important for her future ministry. To the start of her placement, therefore, Rachel brought not only the faith which had led her to offer herself for ministry (her owned theology), but also the theology she was struggling with in college (her learned theology). To use the concepts set out above, Rachel brought to the placement both the story of her own life and her ongoing engagement with the Christian story. All of these would contribute to, and be challenged by, her interaction with the milieu of the psychiatric hospital and the stories of the people whom she would encounter in that setting.

## The College

The College described its expectations of the placement under the headings of purpose and aims for the student. The former was to provide opportunity for theological and social reflection on the experience gained in an urban setting; and the latter that the student should gain experience of the agency's work, examine and evaluate its aims, understand its methods, approaches and skills, and explore the most appropriate model of ministry within it. Additionally students were expected to monitor their own responses to the experience, and to consider the implications of this for their own model of ministry. Implicit within the expectation of the college is the anticipation that Rachel will begin to make some connections between her academic theological studies and her involvement in pastoral care within the psychiatric hospital.

## The Unit

The unit to which Rachel was attached describes its objectives as follows: 'To provide continuity of care and long-term service for people living in the community who have some problems with their mental health'. Patients are allotted to one of three teams on the unit and each team is served by a multi-disciplinary group of staff including psychiatrists, nurses, social workers, psychologists, occupational therapists, a clerical assistant and a secretary. Students of the professions as well as qualified staff make up each team and Rachel joined one team as its student chaplain. The unit is housed in a building which can provide twenty-four-hour-a-day care with residential facilities, as well as day facilities—canteen, workshops, library, launderette, games room and a hairdressing salon. The patients, up to fifty in each team, can live on the unit, attend daily for regular events or just occasionally, depending upon their particular needs, at any time. All are long-term or chronic patients varying in age from early twenties to the seventies, and suffering from a variety of illnesses, schizophrenia, depression, manic depression and personality disorders. Medication, occupational therapy, behaviour therapy and general care and support are the treatments on offer. Rachel was free to work out her own timetable on the unit, which included spending time with the patients involved in the various activities and on their own, and with the staff in meetings and teaching sessions. Each week she had an hour's supervision with one of the chaplains, a Roman Catholic sister.

## The Supervisor

The supervisor had two objectives for the placement. First that it would provide opportunities for Rachel to learn from the experience of being with patients and staff in a psychiatric unit about the giving and receiving of pastoral care. And second, that she would contribute to the chaplaincy service in the hospital by working on this unit and responding appropriately to the unit's needs and requests. Thus Rachel was to be both a worker and a student, and the supervisor was responsible for seeing that both tasks were undertaken, and that Rachel learned and contributed as effectively as possible. To this end she provided Rachel with some general guidelines, arranged to meet her each week to discuss how the placement was developing, and to review her work with particular individuals or groups by way of verbatim reports which Rachel would write up for their meetings. Towards the end of the placement they would together make an assessment of Rachel's work for the benefit of herself and her college.

All these various expectations will contribute to the formation of a 'Learning Agreement' which will be specific to Rachel in this placement. (We shall discuss Learning Agreements in more general terms in Chapter 9). We would expect, however, that the aims and expectations of Rachel, her college, the unit and her supervisor have much in common. For instance, the unit aims to 'provide continuity of care and long-term service . . . to those who have some problems with their mental health'. Rachel feels a sympathy towards such people and believes that God loves them and is somehow with them in their suffering. The supervisor wants to ensure that Rachel learns how to care effectively and to use her beliefs sensitively, and the college wants her to explore the most appropriate ministry in this context. But there are also different emphases and priorities. The unit exists to provide a service to its patients; care and treatment come first and education of those on placement second. The supervisor has to help Rachel find a balance between her role as a worker and her needs as a student. The college wants her to learn about this agency, and also its place in the wider context of an urban setting. Rachel has come not only to satisfy her own interest but also to meet the requirements of those responsible for her training for ordination. The supervisory relationship is the one in which those aims and expectations are to be contained, and in such a way that all the participants are acknowledged and their interests cared for. One concern of Rachel's supervisor will be to provide a context for theological reflection, so that new theological insights may be integrated into Rachel's developing understanding of ministry, in other words provide a setting conducive to the 'collision' or 'intercourse' of narratives.

As we follow the progress of the placement we will see how Rachel and her supervisor endeavour to do justice to these different interests. For the sake of space we will condense their six meetings to four.

### Introduction to the hospital

Rachel arrived at the hospital and met with her supervisor before going to her unit. They discussed some practical matters and the supervisor gave Rachel a brief description of the unit, the names of all the senior members of staff, the guidelines for the placement, and some verbatim forms on which Rachel could record any conversation which she might want to share in supervision. They agreed to discuss supervision more fully at their first weekly meeting. Rachel was very keen to get started and reluctant to spend time exploring her expectations of what lay ahead, so the supervisor let her go. Recalling our diagram of supervision (see page 33) the initial meeting looks like this:

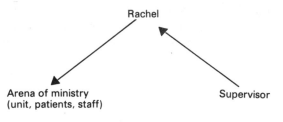

Rachel

Arena of ministry
(unit, patients, staff)                    Supervisor

College

There are links between the supervisor and Rachel and between Rachel and the unit, but the attention is all on the unit. The supervisor tries to explore with Rachel how *she* is but does not engage her in this, and the college is ignored altogether. The supervisor felt some uneasiness about the speed with which Rachel got through their meeting and on to the unit, but if we recall Rachel's own expectations her behaviour has a certain consistency with her aims. She wanted to 'explore' this arena of ministry, and bridge the 'alienating' gap between the sick and the healthy. She is more at home doing things than she is reflecting upon them.

By chance Rachel met her supervisor on the next day, and showed that she was now very anxious. Without prompting she said that she was not sure what she was meant to be doing. The staff on the unit were avoiding her, and not guiding her as she had expected. The supervisor listened, encouraged her to keep going, and said it would be important to talk about this when they met for supervision.

Behind the events of this beginning much has begun to happen. Rachel and her supervisor have coped with the natural anxieties of the beginning of the placement, at least externally, by the discussion of practical issues, guidelines and the names of the members of staff. Beneath the surface Rachel's feelings have been left unaddressed, her corner of the Rhombus ignored. By allowing her to go early, the supervisor has colluded in her flight from emotions into activity. This has repercussions almost immediately when Rachel arrives on the unit before she was expected. Perhaps the staff's response showed something of their anxiety in not being ready for her. Whatever the case Rachel had discovered her feelings; she is anxious and unsure about what she is meant to be doing. The supervisor responds by encouraging her to go on with her experience and to bring her reactions to their meeting. In this way she is trying to help Rachel contain her emotions and use the structure of action and reflection already set out.

**First Supervision**

Rachel arrived promptly for her supervision towards the end of her fourth day, and without reference to her earlier frustrations thrust her first verbatim into the hands of her supervisor. It is the record of a conversation that Rachel had with a thirty-year-old woman called Cynthia, who had been sitting near Rachel in the lounge area of the unit. The supervisor, noting that the conversation was quite a long one, asked Rachel how she would like it handled. Rachel replied that she did not mind, indicating that the supervisor should decide. Sensing that something more than the verbatim was being handed over to her, the supervisor read through the conversation (C = Chaplain, P = Patient):

C1:   Hello, I don't think we've met so far? I'm Rachel, the student chaplain. I'm from the church.

P1:   Oh, (*in a friendly voice*) God is a sore point with me at present.

C2:   Well, see me as a friend. (*pause*). Can you tell me why that is?

P2:   Well, it's my mother you see, she died two years ago, and she was really in pain and having a bad time, and I really thought it wasn't true then.

C3:   You mean that because of your mother's suffering you felt you could not believe in God.

P3:   Yes.

C4:   People often wonder whether God can exist when there is so much suffering. It's an important question. There are no easy answers. I always remember though that God was in Jesus when Jesus suffered on the cross, and that means that God isn't just over there looking on while we suffer, he's actually sharing our suffering with us.

P4:   But my mother was a very kind lady. She would do anything for anyone else. She'd have given her last penny away.

C5:   Sometimes we do see suffering as a kind of punishment and then we want to know why people suffer. Perhaps we've got that wrong? Things do go wrong with people whether they are good or bad. Your mother suffered as well as being a very good lady. Now her suffering is over, and she may well be enjoying great peace and joy now it's passed.

P5:   Do you believe in life after death?

C6:   Yes. I have faith that there is life beyond this one. I don't know whether people pass into a new life when they die, or whether they sleep for a while and wake in a new life. I don't think anyone knows about that, but I do believe that there is a life beyond this one. Jesus believed in and promised new life, and I think he is to be trusted. What do you think?

P6:   Well, I don't know. Like when I asked you about my mother and her pain, I thought it had gone, and I don't know if it has come back.

C7:   Your belief in God?

P7:   Yes, you know when people get cremated do they burn up completely?

C8:   Yes, the ashes can be put in a plot with flowers. Are you asking because you think it affects life after death?

P8:   Yes.

C9:   I think that when we die it is our spirit that lives on. The body decays when it dies but the spirit — the real person — lives on or can live on [this might have been confusing]. Do you belong to a church, Cynthia?

P9:   No, I don't, but I knew a vicar. When my mother died he brought her communion and then she died. She went to a faith healer when she was ill two days before she died, but he couldn't make her well. She expected to get well but she didn't. Sometimes I think I see my mother, do you think that is natural? I sometimes expect to see her just coming round the corner.

C10:  Yes, that's very natural. When people lose someone they love they often see them or expect to see them — it's all part of coming to terms with losing someone you've loved and known a long time. (*Pause*)

P10:  I often go and see my Dad, he doesn't get out much.

C11:  Do you worry about him?

P11:  Well, a bit. I go and see him a lot.

C12:  He lives quite near to you?

P12:  Yes, only round the corner.

(*Seeing that we had covered a lot of ground I decided to draw the conversation to a close.*)

Rachel recorded her feelings at the end of the verbatim by writing that she felt calm, and that the patient had been calm and reflective too: 'I sensed that the conversation could go on too long for Cynthia. I understand her doubts, and do not feel in any haste to be affirming of faith in God. She has to move that step for herself.'

The supervisor drew Rachel's attention to the different view of God that Cynthia held, and suggested that Rachel would have helped her more if she had encouraged her to expand upon her own thoughts and feelings. Cynthia sounded hurt and upset by God, let down by the priest and the healer, and uncertain about life after death and the prospect of seeing her mother again. Rachel might explore all these further with Cynthia. The supervisor also asked her to notice her own need to proclaim the faith, and to share her idea of a God who is with us in our suffering, and asked her to consider whether that was the most effective way to achieve her goal. She kept the verbatim and promised to write some further specific comments on it. Turning to Rachel's experience of the placement, the supervisor asked her about the difficulties she was having at the beginning. Rachel said that she still found the staff rather aloof and unapproachable. Her supervisor suggested that she imagine herself in their shoes. Rachel thought that they might be anxious about her, and in any case too busy to give her much attention. Perhaps they were as much in need of care as the patients, but it had not occurred to her that she could be a chaplain to them as well.

## Theological Reflection

To return to the methods outlined in the last chapter for relating theology to the practice of pastoral care, we observe that Rachel is working at this stage with an 'Applied Theology' model. In handling theological concepts the emphasis has been upon proclamation, though her 'message' has not been about the forgiveness of sins but about the God who is with us in our suffering.

Recalling the Rhombus diagram, all four corners have played a part in this session but the links between them have not been made:

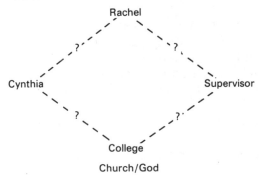

As Rachel says at the start of her conversation with Cynthia, she comes from the church, and she does indeed proclaim its faith. As one might expect, the link between her and where she comes from is the most secure and reassuring, and so dominated her thoughts and responses. The supervisor felt very unconnected to Rachel, and despite her efforts cannot engage with her, which suggests that Rachel may be in some awe of her. Rachel has felt excluded from the unit, and Cynthia's preoccupations about herself and God are some way from those of Rachel and the church.

Rachel has come to proclaim an incarnate faith and yet the experience is one of detachment and transcendence. Theology and practice are split apart from one another, which we saw was a possible consequence of the proclamatory model of pastoral care. Sensing this discrepancy the supervisor endeavours to help Rachel be more present and 'incarnate' by engaging directly with her in supervision and by getting her to imagine herself in the shoes of both Cynthia and the staff.

## Second Supervision

Rachel arrived at her second supervision looking more relaxed and talked easily about her second week on the ward. The staff had asked her to escort a patient out, and she had arranged a short service for the patients. After the service two of them had asked to talk to her and she had agreed, checking first if they were happy to talk together rather than individually. She had given the supervisor a copy of the verbatim before their meeting, part of which follows (C = Chaplain; M = Mary; J = Jane):

C1: Would you like us to talk together or separately?
M1: I'd like us to stay together.
C2: Jane, how do you feel about that?
J1: Yes, I would like us to stay together, but could I have a few words in private after?
C3: Yes, of course, what did you want to ask me?
M2: Well, I go to church and pray a lot. And I think the devil is getting at me, like he never leaves me alone. He gets inside my head and says all horrible things, and makes

me feel I'm a big bad man, and want to go and kill people. And I pray and pray but it keeps on happening and it makes me angry. I was all angry and bad tempered today.

C4: How does that sound to you, Jane? Do you feel the same or different?

J2: Yes, it's like that sometimes. I'm always praying. My church tells me to pray to God to help me when the devil comes like that. But it really gets me down sometimes. I keep feeling sad about my past and remembering sad things.

C5: (*to both*) And when you feel sad about the past Jane, and when you are having all these difficult experiences Mary, where do you think God is? (*Silence*)

C6: When you're coming through these times . . . they are times when you feel vulnerable aren't they? Do you feel God's near or far away?

J3: Near, not away

C7: Yes, I think it's important to remember that God is always with us even when we feel weak and vulnerable. Another thing that struck me when you were talking. Do you know what I mean when I say that to be tempted isn't actually to sin? If we are aware of voices telling us to do things or sad memories, there's a temptation to listen more or get broody. It isn't *sin* to have these temptations you know. And of course (*wanting to hint at their origin in illness*) this hospital and the people here are trying to help us come to terms with these problems as part of illness.

M3: I'll have to tell you about my fridge (here she embarked on a long story about a second-hand fridge which had broken down and caused her a lot of trouble. During it Jane excused herself to go to a class) . . .

M4: . . . the devil was really getting at me with the fridge . . .

Rachel tried again to help Mary see that it was her illness rather than the devil which was causing her to feel so bad. Mary was not convinced, but was appreciative of Rachel's willingness to talk and for the service.

Her supervisor began by affirming her sensitivity in checking with both patients whether they wanted to talk together, and then making sure that both were included and encouraged to contribute. She asked what Rachel felt when Mary began to speak about the devil. Rachel could only remember feeling uneasiness about the teaching she imagined both patients had received from their churches. 'I hesitated to be critical, but it did seem that what they have learnt hinders them from coming to terms with their illness'. 'So you felt some anger too?' the supervisor asked. Rachel admitted that she probably did, saying that she had tried to be constructive first by reassuring them about God's presence, and then by making the connection with their illness. 'How do you think it worked?' the supervisor asked. 'Not very well, I suppose, but I can't see what else I could have done.' 'Was it necessary to do anything, perhaps your listening and the service, as Mary said, was what they most needed and appreciated?'

On the verbatim the supervisor drew Rachel's attention to the importance of both patients' feelings as opposed to the content of what they said. Mary's horror at the devil getting inside her provided a much more vivid picture of her experience than the suggestion that it was just a symptom of her illness. Jane too had sounded a very important note about her sad memories. Perhaps Rachel could encourage her to express more of these feelings.

In this second session a link has begun to be established between Rachel and the unit. They have pulled her in, the staff by involving her in their work and the patients by requesting her time. She too has started to *do* the faith, by having the service, as well as to talk about it, and that has obviously met a need which her proclamation missed. Returning to the Rhombus, a new problem has emerged at the bottom corner. Rachel is troubled by the effect that Jane's and Mary's church is having upon them and of their link with that kind of religious authority. Her strategy is to replace one authority by another. They should believe the hospital and not their religious advisers when it comes to the strange feelings and thoughts they get. The supervisor puts her emphasis behind the link that Rachel has made with the unit and the patients, implying that it is more useful to build on that than to be drawn into a conflict between religion and medicine or one faith and another.

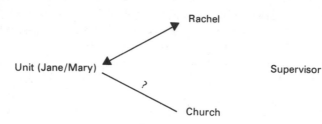

## Theological Reflection

We see at this stage that Rachel is now beginning to work with another model of pastoral care. While elements of the proclamatory model are still present (e.g. C7: 'Yes, I think it's important to remember that God is always with us even when we feel weak and vulnerable'), we see also the emergence of the Applied Psychology or therapeutic model. This is evident at the point (also in C7) where Rachel tells Mary that 'this hospital and the people here are trying to help us come to terms with these problems as part of illness'. This approach leads to another kind of splitting, certainly in Rachel's thinking, for she tried to help Mary see that it was her illness rather than the devil which was causing her to feel so bad. It is possible that Rachel's new understanding of the psychological roots of Mary's illness may stem at least in part from her increased feeling of acceptance in the unit and her acclimatisation to the medical culture.

### Third Supervision

Between the two weeks the supervisor had been wondering how to help Rachel see the effect her preaching style had upon the patients. Last week she had hoped to get Rachel to role-play the conversation with her, Rachel taking the patient's part and she Rachel's, but time had not allowed that to happen and the supervisor felt even more determined to arrange it this week. Rachel had produced a verbatim with a patient called Geoff, which showed some change in her style but also some similar responses. Rachel was rather withdrawn and showed no enthusiasm for the role-play. The supervisor decided not to give in, and although it was a struggle they read the verbatim through together (C = Chaplain, P = Patient (Geoff)):

Geoff is a man in his mid-thirties, the husband of Cynthia, the patient in the first interview. He had joined in the service Rachel organised and then stopped behind to talk with her.

P1:   No, I don't believe in God, I'm not into that.

C1:   Well, it was good to have you with us Geoff. You don't have to believe in God to come. [*I was not sure what he wanted, and although I wanted to clear up, I decided I should wait and see.*]

P2:   No, especially since my mother died of cancer, I've not believed in God or anything like that.

C2:   Mm . . . (*nodding sympathetically . . . I recalled that I had heard something similar from Cynthia*) Did you believe in God before that?

P3:   No, I don't think I did. No, not really. You see I can't stand suffering. There's this man downstairs from me who's a vet and has to put animals down. Well I couldn't do that. I can't even stand the sight of blood.

C3:   You seem to be saying Geoff, that because you yourself could not hurt anyone, you cannot believe in a God who seems to allow suffering in the world. Have I got it right?

P4:   Yeah, that's about it.

C4:   Mm . . . I see. Cynthia wants us to talk about it in the service next week. Perhaps you would like to come and join in.

P5:   Yes, I don't mind. I like that music (indicating my guitar which I play badly!). I like that, it's kind of soothing, it makes you think of things. I think of things in the past. I do a lot of thinking. Things have gone wrong, things I've done wrong. Suffering and all that. My mother dying. It helps me to think of all these things.

C5:   (*nodding in understanding*)

P6:   You see there's a lot of things gone wrong with my life. See, I've been in trouble. Not now, I don't go with children anymore. I just go in the toilet every time I feel like that. (*His manner is strikingly sad, very resigned.*) You see, once I went with a girl, she was out with a dog. She said, I'll take you somewhere where you can tell people your problems. So she took me to this place, and the next thing I knew there were alsatian dogs and the police there and that was it. But I've not done it since. Well it was wrong, wasn't it, you can't blame her . . . I'd like to play the guitar, but I can't read and write you see. It helps me to think like this. Helps me to talk about things.

P6: Is there anyone you can talk to about these things?

P7: No, I can't talk about them really.

C7: Can you talk to Cynthia?

P8: No, I don't talk about these things with Cynthia. No, I don't think there is a God, not unless he appears to me. Not with all these things going on.

C8: You know there are people who go through suffering and also believe in God. What do you think of that?

P9: I don't know really, I don't know about them.

C9: One thing I'd like to say Geoff. When I see the picture of Christ on the cross, it shows God suffering too . . . with us. Does that mean anything to you?

P10: No, not really, But I like the songs. I used to sing the choruses at Sunday School . . . It was good fun singing them.

C10: Well, I hope you will come again and perhaps we can have more songs.

P11: Well, you heard me say I don't believe in God and all that. So, that's good.

C11: Thank you for sharing your thoughts with me so honestly.

Rachel concluded her verbatim with the comment, 'Throughout the interview I have been conscious of not wanting to upset his view of things, only occasionally drawing his attention to things that might enable him to perceive a God who suffers, but not in any way wishing to "convert" him or even, at this stage, change his mind.'

Rachel did not have anything to contribute after the reading of the verbatim. She said she felt sad as Geoff spoke, but did not notice other feelings. The supervisor tried for a while to have her see the different effects of her encouraging Geoff to speak about what he wanted and trying to get him to understand the value of a God who suffers. Rachel could not or would not see it. Eventually the supervisor asked her about what was happening between them. Rachel denied that anything was, so the supervisor asked her how she was feeling at the moment. 'A bit fed up', she said. 'It's not really to do with you. I'm having a bad week. They said on the ward I could take someone to a day centre, and I was really looking forward to it, and then the charge nurse came on duty and said I wasn't qualified to. I think that was the last straw.' 'How do you mean, the last straw?' 'Well, we had this meeting with the college tutor, he's always patronising me and treating me differently from the men. It's probably difficult for you to understand. The Church of England does very funny things to women.' 'I think I do understand, my Church does some strange things too'. Rachel smilingly agreed, 'Yes, I suppose it does'. The supervisor shared some of her experience on another ward, where she had the same sense of being excluded and perhaps not trusted. She asked Rachel what value there might be in such experiences. Rachel looked puzzled. 'Where is God in that kind of suffering, is, I think, your question?' Rachel agreed that he must be there somewhere. 'But he doesn't feel like he's there at all', the supervisor said. 'And anyway, he's another of these "he's" who cause us so much frustration. . . . It occurred to me, Rachel, that your experience has helped you to be closer to people like Geoff. You must have conveyed something of that, for him to share so much with you. I was amazed that you asked him whether he could talk to anyone. He'd just been talking to you, making his confession, and feeling something like an absolution, the thing that only priests can do!'

This session illustrates a lot of the links of the Rhombus being made and the positive effect that has on the supervision itself. First the supervisor sets out to put Rachel in Geoff's shoes and as a consequence becomes much more engaged with Rachel herself. For the first time their supervisory relationship is forced onto the agenda. They have similar frustrations and problems, and that is a great relief to Rachel. She can now safely admit to her negative feelings, for which previously she would have expected criticism. The supervisor makes even more of it by asking her how she can use her frustrations, her suffering. For that was what she came to learn about. This puts her college experience in a new light too, while connecting it to the experience of being devalued in her placement. To cap it all, Geoff has actually used her as an authority, as a minister who can hear confessions and by her openness and presence offer a way to absolution.

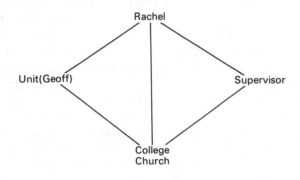

*Theological Reflection*

In this conversation and the subsequent supervision session we see significant changes in the way in which Rachel handles the theological issues. Instead of direct proclamation there is a more gentle kind of exploration. In C2 and C3 Rachel makes her theological statements in the context of a much more accepting relationship and in C5 we find and attempt to reflect feeling, and to understand what Geoff is saying about his belief in God. ('You seem to be saying' etc. . .) The statement in C8 ('You know there are people who go through suffering and also believe in God'), while very sermonic, is followed by an attempt to ascertain what Geoff really feels. She was 'conscious of not wanting to upset his view of things'.

Yet perhaps the most significant evidence of change comes in the supervision session itself. Rachel's experience of feeling rejected by some members of staff has reinforced similar feelings generated by her relationship with a male tutor in college. The fact that Rachel's supervisor is a woman becomes especially important, as they share their common feelings of rejection by a male-dominated Church. Yet, paradoxically, Rachel discovers that her experience has helped her to identify with Geoff in his rejection, and at the same time he has affirmed her as a minister. Her developing awareness of herself as one who can offer a ministry of pastoral care comes not in the pastoral care itself but in the reflection upon it in supervision. Her pastoral identity begins to emerge from the interaction between the story of her own suffering (and that of her supervisor), the story of Geoff's suffering, and her struggle with the story of the God who is both absent from, and present in, the suffering of all humanity.

## Final Supervision

At their final meeting Rachel and her supervisor put together their joint assessment of the placement. Already they had met with staff on the unit to discuss their reactions. This had not been very satisfactory as the staff were under great pressure and could not give much time to it. But that enabled the supervisor to have first-hand experience of Rachel's frustrations, and to help her see that hers was a quite natural and appropriate reaction. It also revealed how Rachel would gravitate, like most helpers, towards those who wanted her, and overlook those who might in fact need her. The staff's aloofness had brought her in touch with her ambivalence about authority in the college and in the Church. It had helped a great deal to have another woman as a supervisor, particularly once she recognised how much they had in common. They agreed that Rachel was more able to assert herself now, and that her sense of autonomy had been helped by their struggle with one another. Rachel said how angry she was with herself for backing away from those in authority. She had always denied that anger; now she thought she could try and use it more constructively. Her style of relating has begun to change too, although she is still anxious if she does not feel in control of a situation. It is hard for her to be told that people in distress may be better off not to be reassured. It hurt to be told that she preaches at people, but it did make sense to see how far her need to relate suffering to God intruded into her conversations, and was always introduced by her. The supervisor suggested that she might like to explore this further in counselling or spiritual direction. (As we show elsewhere, while supervision has certain obvious similarities to both of these helping relationships, it is essentially a different process). The thorough way in which she presented her written work, and the trouble she took over the services, showed her strengths as a pastor. This accounted for the trust in herself, which she creates in other people, enabling them to speak to her so freely and openly. Writing after the placement Rachel summarised her own learning in this way:

> I had to learn to be with patients where they were, often in darkness and confusion, depression and insecurity, and never try to impose my own interpretations or to be directive in a way that was chiefly aimed at helping me feel a sense of achievement. I recognised that this listening involved risk.
>
> It seems that facing up to reality involves facing up to the immense range of problems and maladies that affect mankind, and understanding that God is not far from such things. If God shares what is real about us then he shares with us our despair, frustration, failure, betrayal, sickness and confusion. If that is what is true for us then that is what we offer God. The end of human existence is not a happy, suffering-free life in this world. The mystery of God is that he is with people wherever they are, and their starting point is his. My work on this unit meant some suffering for me too, however comparatively small. I sometimes felt ambiguous, overlooked and unskilled. But we who love God must be where he is, and that may involve a profound risk. It may mean losing ourselves and our security in strange places where we seem to lose touch with all familiar things. I felt this on the unit, unsure of my role, aware of the depths of mental despair around me, shaken by eccentric, aggressive and unpredictable behaviour. I developed a profound respect for the patients and staff of the unit. One young woman I got to know well had a very low opinion of herself. Yet on one occasion I saw her trying to comfort another depressed patient whom everyone else was ignoring. This showed me how important is our response to suffering; it enabled this patient to rise above her own despair.

On the last day of her placement Rachel preached at the hospital service. She said how much she had learnt about suffering not only in the hospital but in the surroundings as well with riots and killings and muggings:

> Believing in God who loves people is not about pretending that suffering doesn't happen. It is about facing up to it. In our reading today, St Luke records Jesus as setting his face resolutely to Jerusalem. All the way along his journey he encountered suffering people. He had brought healing and peace. But the greatest part of his work lay ahead in the suffering of the cross, and he did not shrink from that. Jesus brought honour to suffering and meaning to it, and those of us who suffer share not only in the suffering of man, but in the suffering of God. Jesus' words 'follow me' are an invitation to us to love and serve God in a suffering world, to take up our cross, and to help others carry theirs. I have learnt more about that call and challenge through being with you, and I thank you for that.

So ended Rachel's placement on a psychiatric unit.

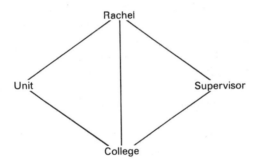

*Theological Reflection*

In describing the theological integration which took place within Rachel during this placement, we wish to use the Whiteheads' schema outlined in the previous chapter. It must of course be recognised that this specific structure was not in the mind of her supervisor as she sought to help Rachel reflect theologically upon what was happening to her. Nevertheless we believe that we do not need to place undue strain on the structure to enable it to act as a framework for understanding what happened to Rachel during the placement.

We see first of all that there are three sets of stories running through the placement: the story of Rachel, the stories of the patients with whom she became involved, and (for want of a better term) 'God's story'. Not only that, we find a common theme running through all these stories, and that theme is 'suffering'.

We hear much about Rachel's suffering. As a sub-plot the story of her great-aunt's suffering in a psychiatric hospital is part of the story which Rachel brings to the placement. As her story unfolds we see that a major theme in it is her own suffering as a woman at the hands of men in both college and Church. The placement brings its own quota of suffering: the feelings generated by being ignored by the staff, being unskilled in the face of great human suffering, and the hurt of being told that she preaches at people.

The patients' stories also become important for Rachel. The stories of suffering told by Cynthia, Mary, Jane and Geoff all make their impact upon her as she tries to be a pastor to them. Further, it was not only the patients who made an impact upon Rachel; she herself through her ministry had some impact upon each of them, becoming an important person in their stories. Though she might have done some things better as far as technique was concerned, to each of them she undoubtedly came across as a caring person, and perhaps as a different kind of pastor from any they had previously encountered.

And the story of the God who suffers is another theme which keeps recurring throughout Rachel's verbatims and supervision. At first Rachel can only handle this theme by preaching about it, but in a way which does not seem to help. All these stories are around without seeming to connect with one another.

In the first two pastoral encounters which she brought to her supervisor, Rachel has worked with both proclamatory and therapeutic models of pastoral care, in neither case very successfully. It is in the third supervision session that something significant begins to happen for Rachel. Her encounter with Geoff and subsequent reflection upon it in supervision become for her what is sometimes described as a 'critical incident.' The breakthrough comes when her supervisor alludes to part of her own story ('My Church does some strange things too'). By sharing something of her own pain, the supervisor enables Rachel both to get in touch with her suffering and to affirm that this suffering has enabled her to get close to people like Geoff. It is at this point that Rachel became free to *attend to* the various stories and really hear them. She also hears for the first time, from her supervisor, an affirmation of herself as a minister in the light of how she was able to hear and help Geoff.

The final supervision session demonstrates how far Rachel has moved. Much has happened between the two final sessions. In the third session Rachel began to listen to the stories, but in the intervening period the stories have begun to interact with one another. This is the second stage of theological integration, the stage of *assertion*, which, according to the Whiteheads, 'instigates a dialogue among those sources of information in order to clarify, challenge and purify the insights and limitations of each.'[18] It must be recognised that this process goes on as much *between* as *within* supervision sessions. The collision of narratives, the intercourse of stories, takes place at both conscious and unconscious levels, in a sensitive process of giving and receiving, each story informing and illuminating the other, bringing to birth a new creation in the form of a changed sense of pastoral identity on the part of the carer.

Rachel's final self-evaluation reveals the outcome of this process. She is now in touch with her own story and able to affirm her strengths despite her suffering, perhaps indeed because of it. She is able to 'hear' the suffering of the patients, developing a profound respect for them as well as for the staff on the unit. The suffering God to whom she bears witness is no longer the compartmentalised deity remote from people, providing an easy security for the preaching pastor, but a God who is now immanent as well as transcendent, a God who may be trusted in the midst of ambiguity and uncertainty. ('We who love God must be where he is, and that may involve a profound risk'.)

We see the third stage of Rachel's pilgrimage of theological integration, the *decision-making* stage, in the sermon which she preaches at the hospital service at the end of her placement. How paradoxical, that for Rachel, the compulsive preacher, her last act of ministry in the placement should be to preach a sermon! Yet the suffering Jesus whom she now proclaims is no longer a docetic Christ, set apart from the realities of human suffering. Her affirmation of her own suffering, her learning from the sufferings of the patients and her understanding of the suffering of Christ on the cross, all come together in a profoundly pastoral sermon. Her theological reflection comes to a focus in a concrete act of ministry. In the light of her new insights she has made a ministerial decision to say certain things in a sermon. She has not said the last word on suffering, but it is her 'Word' for that situation. She will have more to say as her ministry develops for she has not 'arrived'. She has simply entered into a process which will be informed by more pastoral experience and theological reflection.

One final point must be made. We have applied some general principles to the particularities of Rachel's placement. This process will inevitably look very different in other situations. For one thing, the stories will be different, and if they do have a common theme, it may be something other than suffering. Further, the last stage of the process, the *decision-making* stage, will seldom find its focus in a sermon. More likely it will be some further act of ministry, in either the same or a different situation. We believe, however, that the story of Rachel's supervision, in all its uniqueness, may provide a model for making connections between fundamental theological beliefs and the practice of ministry.

## Notes

1. Thurneysen, E., *A Theology of Pastoral Care,* Richmond, VA: John Knox Press 1962, p. 147.
2. Whitehead, J. D. and Whitehead, E. E., 'Educational Models in Field Education', *Theological Education* (American Association of Theological Schools), Summer 1975, p. 273.
3. Thurneysen, op. cit. p. 205.
4. Hiltner, S., *Pastoral Counseling,* Nashville, TN: Abingdon 1949, p. 19.
5. Wise, C., *Pastoral Counseling: Its Theory and Practice,* New York: Harper and Bros 1951, p. 141.
6. Rogers, C. R., *Client-Centered Therapy,* Boston: Houghton Mifflin Company 1965.

7. Niebuhr, Reinhold, *An Interpretation of Christian Ethics*, New York: Meridian 1956, Chapter 4.
8. Luke 24.13–25.
9. Gerkin, C. V., *The Living Human Document: Re-visioning Pastoral Counseling in a Hermeneutical Model*, Nashville, TN: Abingdon 1984, p. 27.
10. This phrase which has come to be especially associated with the name of Boisen seems to have first appeared in his article 'Theological Education via the Clinic', *Religious Education* 25:235, 9 March 1920.
11. Philadelphia: Fortress 1984.
12. Stroup, G. W., *The Promise of Narrative Theology*, SCM 1981, p. 170.
13. Whitehead, J. D., and Whitehead, E. E., op. cit., p. 277.
14. Whitehead, J. D., and Whitehead, E. E., *Method in Ministry*, New York: Seabury 1983, p. 14.
15. ibid., pp. 13–25.
16. ibid., p. 24.
17. Bonhoeffer, D., *Ethics*, SCM 1955, p. 84.
18. Whitehead, J. D. and Whitehead, E. E., *Method in Ministry*, p. 2.

# SIX

# Learning Together

The examples and stories that we have used illustrate something of the complexity and delicacy of a pastor's task. In the last chapter we saw too how a three-dimensional model of supervision provides supervisor and student with some resources for their work together. At one and the same time pastors have to attempt the following. First, they have to give of themselves and their abilities, to be present to those for whom they care and to identify in part with them; to see through their eyes, stand in their shoes and so enter into their story. Second, they have to be aware of their own story too, and of how it affects their reaction to what they hear and see. They have to try to bring from it the understanding and experience which will speak to the stories of those for whom they care. They have by trial and error to find what to offer from within themselves and what to keep unused, and that of course will differ from pastor to pastor, from person to person. And third, they come as the bearers of a much more extensive story, as the representatives of the stories of the gospel, the Church and, ultimately, of God. We saw how difficult a task it is to help students value equally each of these stories or elements and to develop within themselves a pastoral identity which integrates all three. Our gifts, prejudices and experience have us value one more than the others. We adopt a proclamatory or a therapeutic model of pastoral care, or become so absorbed with our own story that we can find little time for anyone else's. The supervisor's task is to help students build upon their strengths and develop those areas which they find most difficult, and also to prepare them for their future ministry, the pressures of which will always make it difficult to attend to, and integrate, the three elements we have identified. So it is not surprising that those who have found supervision an invaluable aid to learning continue to look for support of a similar kind throughout their ministry.

The apostles returned to Jesus, and told him all that they had done and taught. And he said to them, 'Come away with me by yourselves to a lonely place and rest a while.'[1]

The practical nature of pastoral care often draws the carer into intense and personally involving experiences. This 'immanent' and 'incarnate' aspect requires a complementary opportunity for 'transcendence' and standing back in order to look afresh at what was done and said. Thus supervision can be a life-long or ministry-long occasion for telling 'all that we have done and taught'. Some will continue to see it as supervision, and they will seek out those more experienced than themselves to help them in the ways we have illustrated. Others may look for something more mutual, a regular meeting with a colleague or colleagues to consult together about their work. Many of the helping professions now provide this service for their members, both to enhance and develop their competence, and also to reduce the inevitable toll that work of this kind takes on the workers. The needs and demands, distress and deprivation of those who come for care are overwhelming, as is the sense of incompetence, uncertainty, doubt and despair which can arise within the carers themselves. All helpers are at risk of burn-out and break-down, and pastors who are the recipients of so many projections and carry the weight of high expectations are especially vulnerable.[2] There is no way that pastors on their own can keep their work and themselves in proportion. We saw how students under pressure became more rigid and less open to their clients, and more dogmatic and conservative about their beliefs. So too in later ministry all of us can revert to a style of working where the major aim is defence. We will preach and teach and pastor to save ourselves or at least protect ourselves from the growing burden of other people's anxiety and the weight of our own. Such a defence makes for ineffective pastoral care and is in any case a poor protection for the carer, as is revealed by the many personal, professional and spiritual crises amongst pastors and their families. More and more of the Churches' slim resources for care and counselling are being used in response to these crises amongst their work force, and much less attention is being given to the proper and professional support of pastors, which we believe would prevent the inevitable stress of the job resulting in unmanageable distress for the worker.[3] For this reason alone the need to provide consultative services to pastors is urgent if our work force is not to be unnecessarily decimated, and if those who have the skill to support, supervise and consult with colleagues are not to be overwhelmed by the job of salvaging the ship-wrecks and mending the breakdowns.

Those who have a good experience of supervision early in their ministry will move on naturally to use consultation. Others will need encouragement to enter into this process. They are likely to find it as disturbing as did the students in our earlier examples and for the same reasons; but they will have the additional problem of thinking that they should be beyond the need of support by this stage in their ministry. For them consultation with peers and colleagues can be much more acceptable than supervision, because of the mutuality that is implied. Colleagues can help one another, and give as well as receive. Of course this happens in supervision too, but it is not so immediately obvious. Furthermore, in supervision the supervisor has some responsibility for the work of the student and therefore some authority over them. The model of the Rhombus illustrated how these factors could best be acknowledged and then used in the service of learning. In consultation consultants have no responsibility for the work of the consultees or authority over them. They aim only to help the latter do a better job for their clients and at less cost to themselves. That having been said we would like to emphasise the many similarities between supervision as we have presented it, and consultation as we will illustrate it in this chapter.

### Triads: a method of consultation

This method involves three people engaged in ministry who meet regularly to consult with one another about their work. Each member of the triad takes it in turn to have a different role as presenter, receiver or observer. It should be stressed, however, that this is not a role play: the presenter brings some real issue or problem from their current ministry.

The presenter's role is to describe the event, situation or issue with which they want help. The story is told, facts described and feelings expressed. It may be a difficult pastoral problem, a disturbing relationship in the congregation or community, or an administrative problem that never gets resolved. The choice is always the presenter's.

The receiver's role is to provide the best conditions for the presenter to share whatever he or she wants. Using many of the techniques already illustrated, the receiver aims to help the presenter explore the issue or situation as fully as possible. This is done by eliciting feelings, offering possible interpretations, suggesting alternative approaches and encouraging theological reflection. The learning sequence suggested in chapter three, experience-reflection-conceptualisation-experiment, is a useful model for the receiver to keep in mind.

The observer's role is in some ways the most difficult. He or she must remain silent for much of the time, but the role is still crucial to the success of the whole endeavour. The observer has to watch and attend to what takes place between the presenter and the receiver. How is the presentation made? Are the feelings as well as the facts expressed and heard? How does the receiver react, and what effect does that have upon the presenter? What seems to be left unsaid and unacknowledged? Does the receiver intellectualise, reassure, blame or take over the presenter's work? How does the relationship between the two develop? Do they follow the learning sequence or do they omit or over-emphasise any of the stages?

It is important that each maintains his or her role throughout the consultation. The presenter remains in charge of the presentation. It is not the task of the receiver to work with the presentation at one stage removed, nor the observer's to do the same at an even greater distance. The receiver needs to focus not so much on the situation or issue presented, as on the presenter's response to it; and the observer needs to focus on the consulting relationship itself. Whenever the triad meets the roles are rotated so that each participant gains in experience of being presenter, receiver and observer. We turn now to an example of just such a triad. Peter, a hospital chaplain, Mary, a deacon, and Paul, a minister, meet regularly to consult with one another.

This time Peter is the presenter and he wants to talk about a difficult situation in the children's ward of the hospital. He tells the story to Mary as the receiver, while Paul is the observer. Peter is trying to work with two sets of parents, who are on the ward with their very ill children virtually all the time. With the Davidsons he has what he thinks is a good relationship. They talk openly to him about their child's illness; he feels he has been supportive to them; when he visits he knows they want to see him, and when he leaves he always offers a prayer which he feels they appreciate. The Smiths are so different. He just cannot get through to them, and he knows that other members of the staff have a similar difficulty. He can sense the anger when he enters the room, and the staff nurse has told him that she has heard the parents quarrelling. He feels inadequate in his ministry to them. After he has finished this presentation, Mary begins to question him. She wonders why he has told them about both situations. He is not sure. Does he really need help with the Davidsons, or is he ashamed of his failure with the Smiths and includes the Davidsons to make himself feel better? Peter admits to some sense of shame, and agrees that he does really want help with the Smiths. Mary sets out to do this by asking Peter about his feelings for a family with a child the same age as his own. Maybe that stops him hearing their anxiety. Peter looks doubtful, and says that the Davidsons' child is about the same age too, and he is getting on fine with them. Mary is not satisfied and asks him if he is not denying his feelings. Peter remains unimpressed but sinks deeper into his chair. At this point they decide to bring in Paul and see what he has observed to help them understand why they have got stuck. He says that what attracted his attention most was the way that Mary and Peter related to one another, and how it ended with Peter looking beaten and beyond help and Mary frustrated and unhelpful. This reminded Paul of how Peter described his relationship with the Smiths. He could not get through to them any more than Mary could get through to him. He had made her feel as inadequate as the Smiths made him feel. It occurred to Paul that perhaps the Smiths felt a similar inadequacy in the face of their child's illness. Like Peter they might be persecuted by the kind of personal questions and doubts which Mary had raised. Did they feel responsible for their child's illness, and a sense of shame that they could do so little about it? Perhaps that was what they conveyed to Peter beneath their anger. Released from their entanglement Peter and Mary began to contribute to this exploration. In the presence of the Davidsons what else could the Smiths feel but incompetent. And why were the Davidsons so good at managing something which was so difficult for the Smiths? Were they coping *too* well? Mary wondered if the two couples could somehow help each other and be less extreme in their reactions. Paul asked if there was any difference between the two parents in each couple, and Mary interjected that she thought she understood why she had been so persistent in trying to get Peter to admit to his feelings. She said she felt somehow offended by his coolness and dispassionate presentation. Peter said that the Smiths were different from one another. Mr Smith was in control and showed little feeling openly, whereas Mrs Smith looked utterly miserable and withdrawn. Mr and Mrs Davidson appeared to be far more equal. By the time the consultation was over Peter felt able to go back to the ward to try to be more observant of the two families. As Paul had done with them, he would try to see how the couples could be more help to one another. Mary had a feeling that if the two fathers or mothers could relate to each other independently then that might ease the situation.

At their next meeting Mary, Peter and Paul will first review the result of this consultation, and then it will be someone else's turn to present to the others. This simple example illustrates some of the significant features of consultation. The presenter alone is responsible for what he presents and the way he does it. The more freely and naturally he can do this the better. He should resist trying to do it in a way he thinks will please or help the receiver. Rather, he should allow himself to tell it just as it comes, and try to censor as little as possible. The receiver allows herself to be open to whatever comes, as neutral in her attending as possible. She tries not to interfere with questions and comments so as not to interrupt the flow. In letting the presentation come into her she will of course begin to be affected by it. Questions will come into her mind, her own feelings will be affected, and when the presenter is ready she can then respond with her reactions. We saw how literally Mary did this. She reacted to Peter's presentation with as little censorship as possible. This enables the observer to watch the relationship between the others as it unfolds, and to see it alongside the original presentation. Paul began to notice the similarity between what Peter experienced on the ward and what was happening before his eyes. By concentrating on Mary and Peter's relationship and the difficult feelings aroused between them, all three were able to piece together a fuller picture of the kind of feelings which were affecting Peter and his work with the Davidsons and the Smiths. In the earlier chapters we saw how a supervisor attempts to be both the receiver of the student's presentation and the observer of their relationship, and indeed the same is the case for an individual consultant. The advantage in a triad is that the two tasks are separated, and then brought together at the optimum moment for the consultee.

This advantage can be taken further if more people are involved in a consultation. For instance, if there are four participants in a quartet, then presenter and receiver can have an observer each. The observers follow the relationship as it develops from the point of view of the one they are observing, and their contribution when it comes will have this additional perspective. And the presenter and receiver will have the support of someone who has empathised with them. Although it is rarely structured so formally, consultation in a group setting provides many of the same advantages.

## Group Consultation

For many pastors there are considerable advantages in consulting within a group setting. There is the solidarity of meeting regularly with others who face similar problems and pressures and the opportunity to get a variety of different points of view while drawing upon the experience and expertise of a more diverse set of colleagues. If the group can include members of other helping professions, then an even wider set of perspectives can be brought into play. It is, however, important that the members of the group should have enough in common to make their work together possible and be led or helped by experienced group workers. We know of a number of group projects of this kind set up by pastors themselves or by church or denominational authorities, or Health Service institutions.[4] For the most part they will meet regularly with the same members, in order to create the security and trust needed for effective work. In one project a hospital chaplain and a psychiatrist formed a group to help pastors and those working in the community with the mentally ill. In another an Anglican diocese invited pastors themselves to form pastoral support and training groups, whose leaders were themselves supervised in a group setting. Dual leadership is often a feature of such groups. This allows for joint male and female leadership and for the different expertise of a pastor, therapist, social worker or psychologist to be represented. Groups like this give the participants the chance to come and share their work in the ways we have already illustrated throughout this book, and then to make use of the responses and reactions of their colleagues, who in turn will receive ideas and help with their work. Sometimes this will be done quite directly, but more often indirectly via the work done on each others' presentation. The facilitators will seek to help all the participants contribute to, and make the most of, the 'receiver' and 'observer' aspects outlined above. In a group this will happen naturally and without any need to apportion roles as was done above. Individuals will spontaneously identify with different characters and aspects in the presentation; they will have their own examples, hunches and feelings which can all contribute to the work both of the original presenter and of the other members.

We would like to illustrate the kind of consultation possible in a group setting with an example not from one of the groups mentioned above, but from a more structured group exercise. This will reveal quite explicitly what we believe is implicit in any group consultation, as the participants come to identify with different aspects of the presentation, and interact with one another to re-present it again in the group, in such a way as to illuminate the problems and possibilities of the original.

## A Consultation to a Team Rector

The context is a team ministry consisting of Reg, the team rector; David, the team vicar; Susan, a deaconess; and Chris, a deacon. The team covers three former parishes of a mixed but also ageing population. There are three churches; Reg, David and Susan have pastoral responsibility for one each, but they also have special interests and expertise which they share with the whole team. Susan's is worship and spirituality; David's is work and industrial chaplaincy; and Reg's is lay training. Over the last year he has organised a course for bereavement counsellors to help throughout the team ministry with the many who are bereaved. There are now a group of six lay visitors. The team rector has tried to work democratically and delegate responsibilities both within the team and within the churches. The present staff have been together for six months since Chris joined them; the others have worked together for three years, and are about half-way through their contract time. Reg is attending a course on pastoral consultation, and when it is his turn he presents the following situation as typical of his attempts to work within the complex web of relationships in the parish. He has written out from memory a verbatim of part of the team meeting which was given over to considering an issue of his. Susan was acting as chairperson and she it is who starts the conversation (DS = Deaconess, R = Rector, D = Deacon, V = Vicar):

DS1: Well Reg, you wanted to raise an issue about Helen (*a parishioner*).

R1: Yes, it's not very important, but I had a word with Helen the other day, and she mentioned that she was worried about Kate (*another parishioner*). She wondered if we all knew that she was having such a difficult time since her mother's death, and what we might do about it. I must say I hadn't noticed, and thought we really ought to be doing something . . .
(*Silence*)

DS2: I did see her in church briefly the other day . . .

D1: I'm sorry, who are Helen and Kate, I can't put a face to them?

R2: Oh yes, sorry! Helen is one of our natural pastors, she's been through quite a lot herself, but is very sensitive to how others are. Kate . . . difficult to know where to begin . . . Her mother died about three months ago, and she had a very tense relationship with her, and the funeral . . . but really David . . . you know her best. How do you think she is? Is there something we might be doing?

V1: I don't know really, I hadn't noticed anything very different about her.

R3: Maybe we could follow up this lead and send one of the new bereavement counsellors to see her. After all we've finished their training course now, and I think one or two of them could manage this.

DS3: That sounds a good idea. Did you have anyone particular in mind?

R4: Mm . . . I suppose it would be best if it were someone from your congregation David? They would be physically closest, and in touch through the church. Who do you think would cope best?

V2: I don't know . . . who was involved on the course . . . Mrs Wilson perhaps . . .

DS4: She's very involved with caring for her own mother at the moment. Would she have the time?

V3: Yes, that's true. I'm sorry Reg I don't know who to suggest. Who do you think stands out from the course?

D2: I'm still a bit confused. Why is it you want to send someone to see Kate?

V4: That's a good question. It's all rather entangled. You see Kate is quite a strange person, she doesn't fit in very easily. She has this friend Monica . . . well, they live together, at least most of the time they do, and of course that isn't approved of by a lot of people, and Kate naturally gets very upset. She needs all the help she can get . . .

DS5: I'm sorry to cut in but time is getting on. Do you think we can leave this with you Reg to discuss with your counsellor group, who might be the best person, and then they could liaise with David.

R5: Yes fine, I'll do that . . . sorry to have taken up more time than I expected.

The consultation group elected to read the verbatim as the script of a play might be read. Parts were given out, and others were invited to imagine themselves as those not 'on stage' (Helen, Kate, Monica and the bereavement counsellors). After the read-through each of the actors spoke briefly from their role about their reactions and feelings.

### Susan, the deaconess and chairperson of the staff meeting

I was aware of all the business that we had to get through, and wanted to treat Reg's issue as briefly and straightforwardly as he had anticipated. I still feel rather strange being a chairperson among all these men, and with him as 'boss' sitting there. I can't work out whether he has raised this in order to involve us. Is this democracy gone mad? Why doesn't he make up his own mind? Helen is his 'favourite' lay person and he's organised the bereavement counsellors, so he doesn't really need to involve the rest of us at all. I'd better not show that I'm thinking anything like this or it will become very involved, and it will be my fault that the business isn't completed.

### Reg, the rector and presenter of the issue under discussion

(The real Reg was not included in the read-through, and another member of the group took his part.)

I think I am involved in a lot of different things: a) I want to sort this out as quickly as possible, and as clearly as I can, so that everyone knows what is going on; b) I am worried about Helen and how involved she gets; c) I need to find people for my bereavement counsellors to visit. It seemed a good idea organising the course, but I didn't anticipate the problems of finding and matching them with people to visit; d) I don't know what David is up to in this area. I suspect he is more interested in his specialist things than his congregation. Perhaps I can prod him into action; e) Chris is on my conscience for not helping him get to know what is going on. He also irritates me with his questions; and f) Dimly I sense that Kate and Monica are a Pandora's box. Perhaps someone visiting them could keep it firmly shut, at least from Helen's eyes and mine.

*David, the team vicar and Pastor of*
*the church to which Kate goes*

I didn't have any warning of this coming up, and I'm not very
interested in any case. Reg is interfering in my area (working
class estate), both through Helen, and now a bereavement
counsellor (middle class do-gooder) he's going to send me. I
have reservations about all this counselling stuff. It ignores
the wider social and political issues which I believe are at the
heart of the gospel. I will leave it to Reg, but also secretly
hope something goes wrong in order to prove my point. I'm
not proud of that feeling so I deny it to myself.

*Chris, the deacon ordained six months ago*

I wanted to be in this team, because I like a democratic way
of working, and I was very impressed with the ideas and
description Reg gave me about the team. Of course things
have not worked out as I expected. I'm suffering considerable
'ordination shock'. In my confusion and uncertainty about
my role and identity I have adopted the position of questioner
and stirrer-up. I am quite good at asking the difficult questions
and watching the others squirm. It relieves my sense of
squirming inside, and when I do it to Susan and David it
impresses Reg. This is the first time I have dared to do it to
him. The ability and skills of the laity are also a threat to me.
Is there going to be a job for me here at all?

*Helen, the natural pastor who drew*
*Reg's attention to Kate*

I have my own turbulent emotional history, which I have
begun to make more of through the counselling I received
from Reg. I am delighted that he believes in me and is
encouraging me to develop my skill as a pastor. I sense that
he also worries about me and I like his attention, and so I
check out with him what I am doing, to see if he encourages
me or warns me off. I am fascinated by Kate and Monica and
would like to help them, but I need his support and permission
as it is on David's patch. I was a bit surprised and let down

when Reg so quickly took on responsibility for doing
something about it. I shall have to find another 'lost sheep' to
bring to him, which he won't take away.

### Kate, the woman recently bereaved, who Helen is anxious about

I'm really angry with this lot discussing me, saying things are
wrong, and then dishing me out to some stranger to visit.
Who does that Helen think she is? And the clergy, what do
they know about me and my needs? David never takes any
notice, he always wants us to join some campaign or other.
Reg is too busy with people like Helen. Susan can't cope with
Monica and me, probably a latent gay. I like Chris, he asked
the only sensible question. Of course I am in quite a state. My
mother died, damn her, before we'd got things properly sorted
out and before she had managed to ask me about Monica. I'm
really sad that they didn't ever get to talk to one another. It's
partly Monica's fault, she is always so jealous of other people,
and that of course includes the church. I don't know what I
would do if I lost either her or the church, but they always
seem to be at odds in my mind, even if they are not in reality.

### Monica, Kate's friend

Kate always gets us into a mess, she involves too many
people. If she has to go to that judgemental church why can't
she just go and keep her mouth shut? I have no time for
religious people, they think I'm damned anyway, and they try
to destroy our love. Strange isn't it, trying to destroy the thing
they believe in. Now that Kate's mum has gone, I hope we can
really build our relationship. I fear that if we go on in the old
way we will end up destroying one another.

### Bereavement Counsellors in general

We are quite a mixed group who the rector got together to
help with all the visiting that surrounds the funerals in the
parish. There can be as many as three a week. We are keen to
be of help. Those of us who stayed for the whole course
would like to have some counselling to do now, although we

are pretty scared of actually getting started, and luckily no-one has found us anyone to visit yet. We had a nice commissioning service, although it was rather strange standing up and facing the congregation. I bet some of them wondered who we thought we were, some of us wonder that ourselves! This discussion, which of course we would not really know about, is beyond us. One of us could call on Kate, but how would we explain why we've come? After all we've seen her around during the last three months. Wouldn't she think it rather odd if we suddenly turned up? And what would we do if Monica was there too? We didn't role play a situation like this on the course! Let's hope the rector forgets all about it. He is very busy and he can be forgetful.

This disclosure by the characters begins to enlarge the 'play', and as each character speaks the others are all affected and could, and indeed sometimes did, add further reactions, which highlighted more issues bubbling beneath the surface. The group, however, are encouraged not to add anything more, but to let Reg draw out of all that he has heard, felt and thought, what is most striking, disturbing or enlightening to him. His situation has now been enlarged and altered by the free-floating imagination of the 'cast', who do not know the characters they were playing, but are likely to have touched upon some of the unconscious issues which will help Reg understand more of what he has been trying to deal with. First Reg has to cope with the powerful effect this has upon him. He may feel humiliated and ridiculed, and say immediately he is to blame for such a mess. He may be angry and proceed to tell some or all of the characters that they have got their parts wrong, and he will explain how things actually are. So he needs time to let the impact lessen, and to recognise that this was a 'play' based upon his original story, but one that the 'cast' have spontaneously put together and is therefore intentionally *not* the same as his situation. Hopefully it is sufficiently out of focus with reality to show up some things which a more accurate focus would not reveal.

After the role play it is essential that the characters de-role. It helps if this is ritualised in some way, so that the individuals renounce the part they have taken and revert to their own characters and personalities. Then they are free to begin to take notice of the learning which is to be got from the role play. Reg and the group noted a number of things, some of which were immediately helpful, and others which seemed less relevant.

1. Chris's question stood out for everyone, and drew Reg's attention to how it all began with Helen's approach to him. He recognised that he had failed to sense the significance of that, and had treated it like a straight-forward referral. He doubted if the real Helen was testing him out in the way the character suggested, but he knew now that he must go back to her and explore her concern before he did anything else. The group were pleased with this because it reminded everyone of how easily they accepted some referrals at face value, and how often they regretted it later.

2. Reg felt troubled and angry about how the staff meeting was portrayed. As he said, 'I've worked very hard to create an atmosphere of trust and sharing, and you beggars have made me question what on earth I've been up to'. Reg decided not to believe the play totally, but to begin to look at the relationships between the staff, and to try and draw the others out about it. The character who had played 'Reg', said he felt in quite a bind, as though he and the others were not too clear of their relationships with one another. This was echoed by someone else in the group, who said her team had just the same uneasiness about it. As though there was something false about an unequal equality. The theme of being different as well as equal began to make some sense, and Reg felt less isolated with his problem.

3. Someone noted how often people apologised in the play, and wondered if there wasn't a lot of loose guilt lying about tripping everyone up.

4. The middle-class and working-class churches side by side interested Reg. He said he had been aware of tensions but that none of the staff had so far been able to mention them. Perhaps the envy and rivalry among the staff had confused this, and again he thought he would look for a chance to bring it up.

5. The same was true of the sexual issues. On the whole he thought that was going to be more difficult. People wondered about the real Kate and Monica, but no-one knew what kind of relationship they had, and Kate had had a boyfriend until recently. Reg was almost certain that Susan was not gay, but he was sure that she did have difficulty being the only woman in the staff team, and he wondered if things would alter when they were joined by a parishioner currently in training to be a licensed pastoral assistant. Someone asked why she could not join them now while she was training. Reg said that there was no reason, and he would discuss it with the others.

6. That led the person who had represented the bereavement counsellors to ask why they were not included in the staff meeting. Was it because they were not clergy? Reg realised that he must look more carefully at the counsellor scheme, when he could find the time. And some one else asked if he had to do everything himself.

Role play of this kind is an effective way of animating the discussion and exploration which is essential to consultation. It enabled the group to begin to own the story of the consultee and to get to grips with some of the possible underlying issues. They could break out of the stranglehold of objective facts, and have their version of the story (now dramatised) to put alongside the consultee's, in such a way that the two cannot easily be confused. There will always be important differences as well as similarities. Thus the one will throw light on the other, and the consultee can take from it what he finds most helpful. At the same time the group have their version of the story and their enactment in it to apply to their own work, and once again they can take from it what they want. As we saw, a number of members of the role play did identify with the story and the issues, and their own work was enlightened. This gave Reg a sense of solidarity with his colleagues and the knowledge that his work and learning had contributed to theirs.

We hope that these examples have done enough to illustrate how consultation can build upon the foundations established in supervision, and so provide a continuing resource for pastors throughout their ministry. We want now to turn from examples to examine more closely some of the tensions which have been implicit in our illustrations and which we believe are inherent in the task of pastoral care today.

## Notes

1. Mark 6.30—31.
2. Eadie, H., 'The Helping Personality', *Contact* 49, Summer 1975.
3. Walrond-Skinner, S., 'Resistance to the Care for the Carers', *APCC Journal*, no 15, 1987.
4. see Chapter 9 page 155.

# SEVEN

# The Context of Learning

Our concern is with education for pastoral care, with better ways of equipping the people of God for ministry within congregations and communities. While our main emphasis is upon the educational task, we wish at this stage to make clear our understanding of the nature of the pastoral care to which these endeavours are directed. Logically, this chapter might have come much earlier since it could be argued that we should have made explicit our understanding of pastoral care before describing educational methods which may be used in preparing people for this ministry. Yet these issues may also be appropriately addressed at this point as we turn from our consideration of case material to a more systematic presentation of the theory and practice of supervision, with the added advantage that we may refer to this material as we set out the concepts which are central to our understanding of pastoral care.

We have already noted that in the history of the Church, ideas about the main goal of pastoral care have varied from one era to another. We have also been made aware of the model of pastoral care which has been dominant until recent times, that of the 'minister in his parish' exercising a somewhat paternalistic pastoral oversight of his flock.

It is not our intention to devalue previous approaches to pastoral ministry, for each has had its own validity in its particular historical and social context. It should not surprise us, however, if the pastoral care relevant to the late twentieth century has its own modes of expression and self-understanding. Equally, we should expect that while these have a contemporary relevance, the pastoral care appropriate to a future generation will take a different form.

Our current concern, however, is with the forms of pastoral care which seem to be relevant today or in the immediate future. The case histories already set out inevitably contain implicit assumptions about the nature of pastoral care. From the stories of Ian, John, Rachel, Peter or Reg one could easily gain the impression that the essential form of pastoral care is a one-to-one relationship in which someone with expertise offers help to another person with a need or problem. This, however, is a gross oversimplification, as a fuller analysis of these cases demonstrates. While John and Rachel were inevitably involved in one-to-one pastoral relationships in their hospital placements, it soon became evident that their pastoral care of individual patients had to take seriously the wider social context of these individual relationships; this was further developed in Peter's attempt to care for the Davidsons and the Smiths. In the case of Ian we saw that he received from Mrs Brown as much care as he gave to her. Nigel's and Reg's stories uncovered a whole range of interrelated issues within their congregations and communities and a network of inter-professional relationships.

We wish at this point to spell out our understanding of pastoral care and make explicit those assumptions which are implicit both in our handling of the case material and the related theoretical discussion. It is our contention that the concepts of pastoral care which make sense at the present time may be expressed in terms of a number of tensions or polarities. These are:

1 The tension between pastoral care as a response to human crises and pastoral care which is concerned with the development of human potential within the community of faith.

2 The tension between pastoral care which is rooted in the faith and mission of the Church and pastoral care which is informed by the insights of the human sciences.

3 The tension between pastoral care which is the function of the whole people of God and pastoral care exercised by women and men trained and set aside to exercise special functions within the Church.

4 The tension between pastoral care which is spontaneous, and is characterised by a mutuality of giving and receiving

on the part of carer and cared for, and pastoral care which demands training and skill.

5 The tension between pastoral care concerned with the wellbeing of individuals and pastoral care which takes seriously its social and political context.

6 The tension between pastoral care which has its own integrity and pastoral counselling which is but one aspect of pastoral care.

An understanding of these tensions within contemporary approaches to pastoral care is fundamental to the practice of supervision, whose objective must be to enable learners to locate each act of ministry within such tensions. These polarities constitute a map of the territory within which ministry will have to chart its course and learners will need to find their own place within each of these tensions. Supervision will seek to prevent distortion or diminution in ministry resulting from an innate tendency to identify consistently with one set of polarities: for instance a crisis ministry to individuals entirely dependent upon secular psychotherapy, or a ministry of social action which ignores the needs of individuals or sees deep human need simply in terms of the theological concepts of sin and salvation without any reference to modern personality theory.

Let us now examine each of these tensions in turn.

## 1 Crisis and growth

Pastoral care has frequently been perceived as a helping response to the crises of life, and so it is. Those with any experience of ministry will have spent much time and energy supporting people who are shattered by bereavement, or worried by the onset of illness, or deeply troubled by the break up of their marriage. All this is taken for granted. A pastoral ministry which does not respond with compassion to those human crises is a contradiction in terms. Yet an understanding of pastoral care which sees itself solely in these terms is impoverished and defective. We may presume that while Jesus left the ninety-nine in the sheepfold to go in search of the sheep that was lost, his concern for the lost sheep did not imply any abandoning of his commitment to the long-term welfare of the rest of the flock. When the lost sheep had been found, no doubt the good shepherd returned to the routine work of tending the whole flock.

This, as we have already noted, was a major insight which the late Bob Lambourne contributed to the development of pastoral care in Britain. When discussions were taking place which led to the formation of the (British) Association for Pastoral Care and Counselling he wrote a paper warning against an approach to pastoral care which was no more than 'problem-solving'. For Lambourne pastoral care consisted of far more than the 'elimination of defect' in which the dominant mode of ministry is psychotherapy or counselling:

> Pastoral care, of which pastoral counselling is a part, is separated from its very life unless it is substantially concerned with the continual renewal of the holiness-in-service of the Church as *koinonia* rather than be preoccupied with ego-formation identity righteousness or salvation of its individual members.[1]

Thus Lambourne advocated an approach to pastoral care which was concerned with something more than helping individuals negotiate the crises of life, and more even than growth conceived of by much of the human potential movement.[2] Throughout his teaching and writing there is a concern for pastoral care directed towards helping women and men realise their full potential as human beings within the community of faith, as much as with helping individuals solve their personal problems. It is also possible that the problems of an individual may be symptomatic of the system or systems of which that individual is a member. In the story of Ian's ministry to Mrs Brown we know nothing of her relationship with her family, friends, church or community. Further pastoral care for Mrs Brown would, of necessity, involve an exploration of her place within these networks of relationships, to see if there were any factors, such as family tensions, exacerbating her grief, and what resources were available to support her through the crisis and help her find a new role for herself.

Other writers have also made explicit the importance of both the 'faith' dimension and the corporate dimension of pastoral care. Frank Wright in his book, *The Pastoral Nature of the Ministry* emphasises the former. He eschews any superficial distinction between the minister and the secular social worker on the grounds that the former is either more highly motivated or more richly sustained, but argues that the explicit task of the minister as pastor is to 'keep the mystery of God present to man', not in terms of what he does or says but simply in terms of being:

> In days when there are so many words of counsel and good advice, it is perhaps only when we stop striving and look around and attend that the mystery can be present.[3]

We see the broader, corporate conception of pastoral care in the work of the American psychiatrist Mansell Pattison, who has written of the need to develop a systems approach to pastoral care, an approach which draws its inspiration from community psychiatry rather than individual psychotherapy.[4] He sees it as the primary task of the pastor to develop the Church as a social system unique in its concern for people. The Church is a centre of moral dialogue, a fellowship where men and women can be accepted with their frailty and vulnerability, a learning arena where they can grow in their understanding of others, themselves and God, and a worshipping community where God's grace and forgiveness is proclaimed and experienced, and so uniquely placed to be a centre of growth and renewal.

Thus the first polarity which we identify in our contemporary understanding of pastoral care is one which holds in tension a traditional approach, focusing on support for individuals in crisis, and a broader approach which emphasises the building up of the Church as an arena where men and women can grow in faith, hope and love. It will be obvious that these polarities are not mutually exclusive but are two sides of one coin, each essential to the existence of the other. We see these objectives at least partially fulfilled in John's ministry among the old people in hospital as it broadened from a personal concern for one or two individuals to embrace an understanding of the culture of the whole ward and of the needs of the staff. This too is implied in Reg's work with his team, and in Mary's suggestion to Peter that he encourage a mutuality of care between the Smiths and the Davidsons.

## 2 Theology and the Human Sciences

There is a tradition of pastoral care in the Church with a literature stretching back to its origins. Thomas Oden has examined the use made of these classical theological resources by representative authors in the field of pastoral care in the nineteenth and twentieth centuries.[5] His conclusion is that while nineteenth-century writings contain numerous references to the work of Augustine, Chrysostom, Luther, Calvin, Richard Baxter and others, books written in the mid-twentieth century are totally devoid of references to this classical tradition. He further shows that these same textbooks on pastoral care are heavily dependent on contemporary writing on psychotherapy, such as that of Freud, Fromm, Rogers and Berne.

Oden's work highlights an important issue in the contemporary debate about the nature of pastoral care, namely the relative importance of the contributions of theology and the social sciences to our understanding and practice of pastoral care. We have already referred to a polarisation within the theology of pastoral care. While a 'proclamatory' model has seen pastoral care as an expression of the Church's call to preach the gospel, the 'therapeutic' model has found its theoretical base and modalities in the secular psychotherapies. More recent publications emanating from North America, while affirming the contribution of the social sciences to pastoral care, have also sought to recover the theological roots of the discipline. A particularly good example of this trend is John Patton's *Pastoral Counseling: A Ministry of the Church.*[6]

In the account of Rachel's placement we looked at other ways of relating theological insights to the practice of ministry. Rachel both began and ended her placement with some attempt at proclamation. Yet her preaching at the final service had a very different quality to it compared with the anxious 'God-talk' of her initial conversations. During her placement she learned to listen not only to the patients but also to herself and her final sermon was preached out of herself and the situation and not imposed upon it. In this kind of preaching the gospel is seen not as an alternative to therapy but as complementary to it. While we do not see pastoral care primarily as a means of evangelism, we affirm a conviction that there is nothing so profoundly evangelical as good pastoral care.

## 3 Ministry and Laity

The tension here is between one view which regards ministry as the sole prerogative of a special group of people within the Church, normally ordained ministers or other professionally trained workers, and another view which sees ministry as belonging to the whole people of God. We have already noted an attitude which consciously or unconsciously devalues the pastoral care offered by anyone other than 'the minister'. Yet this is an attitude which is neither biblically based nor informed by a theological understanding of the nature of ministry. Our assumptions are first of all that the primary ministry of the Church is that of Jesus Christ himself; secondly that all Christians are called to share in that ministry; and finally that there are some women and men who are called, trained and commissioned to exercise certain special ministries within the one ministry of Christ and his Church. This is a view of ministry which we believe to be congruent with the vision of the Church set out by St Paul in 1 Corinthians 12, which identifies the diversity of gifts within the one body of Christ.

We shall affirm a theology and practice of ministry which does not see the ordained ministry as exercising a kind of pastoral care different in nature and isolated from the ministry of the whole people of God. Yet at the same time it recognises the distinctive contribution of an ordained and/or commissioned ministry within the life of the Church. There is one ministry shared by 'ministry' and 'laity'. Neither must be devalued at the expense of the other for they are interrelated and interdependent. There are important and distinctive ministries, which are integral to the Christian vocation of many people within the Church, and are exercised by elders, class leaders, churchwardens and countless others in

congregational and community life and in work situations.
Nevertheless, there are also some within the Church who, by
virtue of their office, appointment or training, are called to
exercise certain ministries on behalf of the Church. These
latter ministries consist not only of direct pastoral care of
individuals and groups, but also involve a supportive role in
facilitating the ministry of others.

This is evident in the case study in which Reg, the team
rector, not only exercises his specialist ministry, but also
assumes responsibility for training and supervising a team of
lay bereavement counsellors who have a distinctive ministry
within the congregation. We shall observe too a broader
dimension to Reg's ministry in his style of leading the team of
professional church workers for whom he has administrative
responsibility. To be aware of individual ministries within
the congregation, each with its own distinctive function, is
not to devalue any of them but to affirm their richness in
diversity.

### 4 Mutuality and expertise

We have noted the mutuality which must characterise genuine
pastoral care. We saw this in the case of Ian who in the
course of seeking to care for a bereaved lady found himself on
the receiving end of her care and concern. Yet while
acknowledging the mutuality which is inherent in caring
relationships, the very fact that we are engaged in a study of
pastoral education points to the fact that there is more to be
said.

The issue is complex and leads us into the area of
motivation in pastoral care. Those who seek to care for others
seldom fail to receive something in return, even if it is no
more than the satisfaction of having tried to help another in a
time of need. The 'need to be needed' is a characteristic of
many, if not all, who seek to care for others. Yet if the
overriding motivation for seeking to care is a conscious or
unconscious need to receive care, the would-be carer will do
little good and possibly much harm.

At this point an important dimension of pastoral education
becomes evident. Those who would be involved in caring for
others at a deep personal level must be enabled to realise the

often conflicting motives which lie behind their desire to help. Rachel was in touch, at least in part, with the factors in her personal and family background which led her into this work. The experience of having a great-aunt who required a prolonged stay in a mental hospital was part of Rachel's story, and motivated her to consider a ministry to those who suffered from psychiatric illness. In this ministry some of her own needs were being met, needs which had their origin in the complexities of her earlier family life. Rachel 'needed' to care for the mentally ill and in so doing she received a degree of satisfaction. Yet as well as this subjective dimension to mutuality in pastoral care it is also possible to identify, on occasion, a more objective one. No one who has been involved in ministry for any length of time can fail to be aware of situations where having gone to offer help, one comes away strengthened by the faith and courage of the person supposedly in need of care.

The dimension of mutuality in pastoral care must never be lost sight of. Yet it cannot be total. Irene Bloomfield, a psychotherapist, writes:

> If there is an expectation of total mutuality, the relationship is one of friends and neighbours, but it is precisely because friends and neighbours have not been able to give what was needed that people feel the need to consult a professional.[7]

Along with the mutuality which characterises pastoral relationships we must also recognise their essential asymmetry. In a book on pastoral care in terminal illness, Bruce Rumbold describes the helping relationship as possessing an 'asymmetric mutuality'.

> This indicates both the differing roles of therapist and client — other examples of asymmetric mutuality are mother and child or teacher and student — and the fact that the goal of their relationship is mutual growth and trans-formation. . . . In this sort of relationship there is negotiation and sharing of control.[8]

In pastoral care the differences of role are both symbolic and functional and may be understood in terms of certain expectations, or projections, which are invested in the carer.

These may be either positive or negative but must be carried by the carer for the sake of the other.

Consider the situation where a hospital chaplain visits his bishop while the latter is a patient in the hospital. The normal working relationship of bishop and priest might be described as one of asymmetric mutuality, for in their shared ministry within the Church the bishop has authority over, and care for, the priest. Yet in this particular set of circumstances in which the bishop is patient, there is a shift, almost a reversal, in the asymmetry of their relationship. The chaplain as priest must now be pastor to his bishop, who invests in the chaplain, and expects him to carry, the authority for that ministry, an authority which he must carry not for his own sake but for the sake of the one to whom he ministers.

The process of pastoral education therefore requires a developing awareness not only of the different dimensions of mutuality which belong to the pastoral relationship, but also of the subtle asymmetry which may exist within that mutuality.

Closely related to the tension between expertise and mutuality is that between training and spontaneity. This tension recognises that, on the one hand, much real care is a spontaneous, unpremeditated outreach of one human being to another and, on the other hand, that pastoral care exercised on a regular basis in the context of an intentional ministry cannot be wholly spontaneous but requires an inbuilt capacity for reflection upon that ministry. John's story illustrates this development. His initial enthusiasm just to care is broadened considerably as he is helped to reflect upon the way in which he cares.

Heije Faber in his classic study *Pastoral Care in the Modern Hospital* compares the role of a minister in hospital with that of a clown in a circus.[9] The clown has his own unique and essential role in the circus introducing a dimension of humanity amidst the amazing feats of the lion-tamers and the trapeze artists. Similarly a minister in a hospital can be seen as another human being with whom patients can identify in the midst of all the high technology. Faber works out this similarity in terms of three tensions of his own:

First the tension between being a member of a team and

being in isolation; secondly the tension of appearing to be and feeling like an amateur in the midst of experts; finally the tension between the need for study and training on the one hand and the necessity to be creative on the other.[10]

Our concern here is with Faber's third tension. In all true caring there must be an element of the unpremeditated, of one human being reaching out to another. If pastoral care becomes too professional, it can degenerate into an approach to people which is cold and mechanical, relying on a technique which is devoid of warmth. Yet as Faber points out there is another side of the picture:

> If the minister is to be compared with the clown, he is not to overlook how Grock, one of the greatest of the clowns, would study his act almost daily, frequently giving it fresh slants, and taking care to note the reactions of the audience. He realised that the clown had to be professional. The pastoral ministry is also a trade one has to learn and make one's own by study and training.[11]

Again, this is a tension which cannot be resolved in terms of an 'either/or'. The aim must be to enable pastors to use the skills of their trade in the midst of spontaneous and open relationships, to be aware of what they are about, but, paradoxically, 'forgetting' the skills, which become second nature, like riding a bicycle. Good intentions which lack critical self-awareness, or an easy expertise which is devoid of spontaneity and warmth are both insufficient to sustain a ministry. The aim of pastoral education must be to marry an innate disposition to care with the acquisition of skills and understanding, a relationship which we believe may be forged through the processes of pastoral supervision.

## 5 The personal and the political

Another tension in the debate concerning a contemporary understanding of the nature of pastoral care may be expressed in terms of the following questions. In seeking to care for people in times of personal distress or in helping them attain their full potential as human beings within the life of the Church, is it not possible that we are ignoring a matter of fundamental theological and practical importance? Is it not possible that we are simply helping people to adjust to society as it is, when in fact the purpose of the Church and its ministry should be the transformation of society? Might it not also be argued that in seeking to help people in trouble and ignoring the social and political factors which are at least partly responsible for their troubles, we are embarking upon a course of action which is at best palliative, and at worst useless or even irresponsible? What is the point of seeking to give emotional support to someone who is unemployed while turning a blind eye to the political roots of unemployment? Can there be integrity in a pastoral ministry to the victims of discrimination, whether racial or sexual or any other, which does not seek to change the social attitudes which lead to such discrimination? David in Reg's story would probably have held views like this, as might Monica and Kate.

These issues are not peculiar to ministry but have parallels in other professions whose aim is to respond to human need. Thus Alastair Campbell writes of 'the two faces of social work' when he explores the tension between the traditional 'personalist' emphasis in that discipline and its radical critique.[12]

It must be recognised and affirmed that both care for the individual and social action have a central place in the life and mission of the Church. While they may not be identical in their short-term objectives, they are interdependent, with long-term goals relating to the establishment of the kingdom of God. In his book *Liberating God: Private Care and Political Struggle*, Peter Selby writes:

> Many who begin by being drawn into acts of individual compassion or by assisting others to come to terms with their inner difficulties are brought quite quickly into a concern for the roots of those difficulties. Others begin by campaigning then discover the need to cultivate the inner resources necessary to non-violent resistance or to channel their anger in appropriate directions. The inner and outer struggles may look different but they are both struggles for the triumph of love over hatred and hope over despair.[13]

What are the implications of this discussion for pastoral education?

First, if care of individuals and social action are not identical, then education for these differing facets of ministry must not be prosecuted without an awareness of their interdependence. Nigel and Rachel's stories point in the direction that caring for individuals is not enough, and, further, that heroic attempts to do this uncover the inadequacy of our social structures in caring for those most vulnerable in our society. It must be admitted that much pastoral care has proceeded in isolation from its social, political and moral context. It is the psychological equivalent of an evangelical piety which assumes that one can change society simply by saving souls, or, worse, that if souls are saved, society does not matter. It must also be recognised, however, that there is a kind of social activism which tries to change the world while ignoring the complexities of the human factors involved. The transformation of society demands not only an understanding of the attitudes and resistance of those affected by change, and of the powerful forces at work within groups and communities, but also some self-understanding on the part of those who seek to bring about change.

Second, while care for individuals and social action are both integral to the life of the Church, and mutually dependent, it is also possible that these different ministries may attract different types of people. There should be frank recognition of the variety of ministries within the Church. Further, each ministry demands its own training and expertise, and it is unrealistic to expect omnicompetence or unlimited time on the part of all who engage in ministry. Provided there is mutual sensitivity and appreciation this should be accepted. This is not to deny that there will always be people who will have a personal commitment both to pastoral care of individuals and to social change. Peter Selby identifies those whose pastoral practice leads them inexorably on to political activism. Further, the good care of individuals may well provide that degree of internal freedom which makes some people effective agents of change in society.

Finally, while individual pastoral care and social action have their own strategies and methods of training, the educational processes which can prepare people for these ministries may not be altogether dissimilar. One of our major concerns is the supervision of learners in different kinds of placements. Recent developments in theological field education in the United States have included placements in social action ministries as well as in more conventional pastoral settings. Hunter describes a student placement in a social action ministry in Boston:

> The purpose of this project is to provide an opportunity for students to have a professional experience in the social action dimensions of the Christian ministry. The project is designed to develop professional competence specifically in the area of influencing legislation dealing with a variety of social issues such as prison reform, low-income housing, education, welfare, health care and government reform.[14]

He goes on to describe how students are supervised in their task of influencing legislation in the decision-making centres of the country. This includes work on their own vocational understanding as it relates to the role of the clergy and Church in influencing public policy.

## 6 Pastoral care and pastoral counselling

An important feature of the development of pastoral ministry in the twentieth century has been the growth of pastoral counselling as a specialist ministry, sometimes to the extent that it has developed in isolation from the main stream of church life, with many practitioners finding their professional identity as pastoral counsellors rather than as ministers. Recent writings, however, would seem to indicate that pastoral counselling is rediscovering its ecclesiastical roots. Thus John Patton sets both pastoral care and pastoral counselling in the context of the Christian community's response to persons who in some way are alienated from their faith and from other people. The difference between them is that

> in pastoral counselling the roles of the primary giver and receiver of care are much more clearly defined than in pastoral care, and the alienated person has taken initiative to seek the help which he or she needs. It may include support, guidance and a variety of other means through which care may be expressed.[15]

Pastoral counselling, therefore, is an important specialist ministry of the Church and the great contribution which such specialist ministries make to helping people in need cannot be denied. Our approach to pastoral education, however, rests upon the conviction that pastoral care has its own integrity. It is necessary, therefore, to clarify further the differences between pastoral care and pastoral counselling, not least in order to safeguard the integrity of each. Pastoral care as understood in the context of the present discussion covers a very broad canvas. It encompasses much, but not all, of the everyday work of a minister in the midst of a congregation and parish; it includes visits to a newly-bereaved family and follow-up visits after the funeral, visits to members of the congregation in hospital, and to the elderly and housebound. It takes in the apparently casual encounters with worshippers after services, and the conversations which occur at a coffee morning. Another book in the New Library of Pastoral Care series points to the opportunities for ministry presented by baptisms, weddings and funerals.[16] The same may be said for worship. Using the insights of pastoral care and pastoral psychology, William Willimon asserts that true pastoral care cannot take place apart from an active worshipping community of faith, and that pastors can find a rich source of ministry in their role as leaders of worship.[17] Preaching itself will frequently have a pastoral dimension, and any course of social action which is rooted in the gospel will have at its heart a concern for people.

Further, as we have seen, pastoral care extends far beyond the work of the clergy; in the life of the local congregation, pastoral care includes the befriending and support offered by many lay people who share in the visitation of the elderly and sick, and in countless acts of human care and concern which need no label. For a hospital chaplain, pastoral care involves both the systematic visiting of wards and the brief bedside visits to patients and their families in a time of crisis, as well as the more extended counselling of patients who are specially referred. Drinking coffee with staff during a crisis or in more relaxed moments is an expression of pastoral care, as well as the interviews in depth with a nurse who has come to talk about her disintegrating marriage.

What then are the differences between pastoral care and pastoral counselling?

(a) In pastoral care, the initiative is usually taken by the carer. A minister does not normally wait for an invitation to visit a bereaved family, indeed a visit is expected. The privilege of initiative built into the pastoral role is one of the features which sets ministry apart from most other caring professions and is often the subject of envy by them.

This is evident in virtually all our case studies. Ian's visit to Mrs Brown, John and Rachel's conversations with patients in their respective hospitals and Peter's care of the Smiths and the Davidsons, are all examples of a pastoral care which springs from the pastor's freedom to initiate relationships. In pastoral counselling, however, the initiative is normally taken by the person seeking help who, perceiving that the minister may be able to provide some support, makes the first approach.

(b) In pastoral care, the relationship is generally unstructured, particularly with regard to space and time. This means that in pastoral care there is frequently a *kairos*, an opportune moment, which if not perceived when it occurs, may never happen again.

Pastoral counselling is generally more structured. While pastoral care is not the same as pastoral counselling, counselling may be seen as a specialised kind of pastoral care, and frequently what begins as pastoral care may develop into a counselling relationship of considerable depth. When it becomes apparent that this is what is happening, it is then generally advisable to provide a more structured setting for this deeper kind of exploration. This is preferable, not only so as to provide a place where the conversation can proceed in privacy and without interruption, but also in order to set boundaries to contain the deeper interactions. We saw how Rachel's ministry of pastoral care soon developed into counselling as patients began to seek her out. When this happened it was appropriate that she should begin to give more structure to her pastoral relationships. So when Mary and Jane asked to talk with her, she immediately asked them 'Would you like us to talk separately or together?'

This issue of structure is closely related to that of initiative discussed above. If pastoral counselling is characterised by greater depth, this is perhaps another way of saying that in counselling there is likely to be a greater emphasis upon unconscious processes. By contrast, pastoral care will tend to focus more upon the conscious forces at work in the pastoral relationship. In order to deal with unconscious material, a more clearly defined contract must be negotiated between the parties involved, and it is easier to establish this kind of relationship when the initiative comes from the person seeking help. It is one thing to initiate pastoral care, it is something else to confront the different forms of resistance which inhibit personal growth. In a counselling relationship, on the other hand, it may be possible, if not essential, to deal openly and honestly with such resistance.

To distinguish between pastoral care and pastoral counselling simply on the grounds that one deals with conscious processes while the other deals with the unconscious is of course a gross over-simplification. Every pastoral care relationship is almost certain to be influenced by unconscious factors. We are alluding here to the phenomenon of transference which, as Howell points out, while it has its roots in psychoanalysis has a general application to all helping (and indeed all human) relationships:

> . . . the patient, mainly unconsciously, displaces onto the analyst emotions which were earlier felt in relation to some other significant figure in the patient's life, such as a parent. The analyst is felt about, and in some sense perceived, as if he or she were this other figure in a form which had become lost in the unconscious.[18]

Later Howell writes:

> Pastoral care and counselling often evoke responses which may seem inappropriate and may be confusing, alarming or provoking, especially if they are sexual or aggressive. A general understanding of transference theory and manifestations can help maintain the degree of detachment and emotional containment needed in such circumstances.

It is for this reason that some training in counselling is so valuable for all who are to be involved in ministries of pastoral care. While in the normal course of pastoral relationships it may not be appropriate to explore unconscious factors, it will help enormously to be aware of their existence.

(c) While pastoral care normally occurs within the complex network of relationships which constitute the life of a congregation, this may not be the best framework for pastoral counselling. This does not mean that a minister should never be involved in a counselling relationship in depth with a member of his or her own congregation; often this takes place with great effectiveness and there may be no viable alternative. Nevertheless, before embarking on such a relationship certain questions must be considered by the pastor. Is the minister of a congregation, to whom a member relates in many different ways, the best source of help, or would it be better to talk to a stranger? There is also the question of competence. While every minister must be skilled in offering a ministry of pastoral care, it is generally recognised that counselling demands a different kind of training and, further, that training in counselling does not necessarily provide the best preparation for ministry. There are other resources in the community of a more specialised kind such as marriage or bereavement counselling and a major pastoral skill is the art of referral, something which needs to be done so that the one who is referred does not feel abandoned by the pastor.

We see therefore that any contemporary understanding of pastoral care will be far from simple. Both the realities of the pastoral situation and the psychological and theological understandings of each pastor, whether lay or ordained, will shape the practice of ministry. What is important is that pastoral education should provide the map which will enable those engaged in ministry to find their way through the territory with some awareness of their bearings.

## Notes

1. Lambourne, R. A., 'Personal Reformation and Political Formation' *Contact* 44, Spring 1974, p. 31.

2. Rogers, C. R., *On Becoming a Person,* Boston: Houghton Mifflin Company 1961; Perls, F., Hefferline, R. F., and Goodman, P., *Gestalt Therapy,* Pelican 1973.
3. Wright, F., *The Pastoral Nature of the Ministry* SCM 1980, p. 10.
4. Pattison, E. M., 'Systems Pastoral Care', *Journal of Pastoral Care* XXVI; 1 March 1972, pp. 2—14; also *Pastor and Parish: A Systems Approach,* Philadelphia: Fortress 1977.
5. Oden, T., 'Recovering Lost Identity', *Journal of Pastoral Care* XXXIV; 1 March 1980, pp. 4—19; also *Care of Souls in the Classic Tradition* Philadelphia: Fortress 1984.
6. Patton, J., *Pastoral Counseling: A Ministry of the Church,* Nashville, TN: Abingdon 1983.
7. Bloomfield, I., 'Counselling and Consultation' *Contact* 60, 1978: 3, p. 19.
8. Rumbold, B. D., *Hopelessness and Hope,* SCM 1986, p. 39.
9. Faber, H., *Pastoral Care in the Modern Hospital,* SCM 1971, pp. 84—92.
10. ibid., p. 81.
11. ibid., p. 87.
12. Campbell, A. V., *Moderated Love: A Theology of Professional Care* SPCK 1984, Chapter 4.
13. Selby, P., *Liberating God: Private Care and Public Struggle,* SPCK 1983, p. 6.
14. Hunter, G. I., *Theological Field Education,* Boston Theological Institute 1977, p. 101.
15. Patton, op. cit., p. 16.
16. Carr, W., *Brief Encounters: Pastoral Ministry Through the Occasional Offices,* SPCK 1985.
17. Willimon, W., *Worship as Pastoral Care,* Nashville, TN: Abingdon 1979.
18. Howell, D. D., 'Transference' in Campbell, A. V., ed., *A Dictionary of Pastoral Care,* SPCK 1987.

*Further Reading*

Deeks, D., *Pastoral Theology: An Inquiry,* Epworth 1987.
Pattison, S., *A Critique of Pastoral Care,* SCM 1988.

# EIGHT

# The Learning Laboratory

The accounts in the first six chapters illustrate among other things how significant a feature anxiety is to pastoral care and the supervision of it. The story of the good shepherd in St John's Gospel introduces this theme with the thieves and robbers who are expected to break into the fold, and the hirelings who will leave the sheep unprotected.[1] In contrast the good shepherd, like the door of the fold, places himself between the sheep and danger. In a similar way, pastors seek to protect those for whom they care, and in particular to help them manage their anxiety constructively, so that they can indeed live their lives and live them abundantly. As pastors aim to contain and enfold those for whom they care, so also their supervisors try to contain the anxieties induced by that activity and to help foster the freedom within that containment which enhances life and fulfilment. The aims of both supervision and consultation are to enable the recipients to use their anxiety as effectively as possible in the interests of those for whom they are caring, and as a means for their own professional development. The process of helping individuals acknowledge and then use their anxiety is analogous to the relationship of parents helping their children negotiate the anxieties of growing up. Winnicott describes the maturing of children from their total identification with their mother at birth to their separation and growing independence within the first year of life. He identifies the key function as one of 'holding':

> Holding is very much related to the mother's capacity to identify with her infant. Satisfactory holding is a basic ration of care, only experienced in reaction to faulty holding. Faulty holding produces extreme distress in the infant giving a basis for the sense of going to pieces, the sense of

falling apart, the feeling that external reality cannot be used for reassurance and other anxieties that are usually described as 'psychotic'.[2]

The 'good enough' mother is able and willing to give support and protection to the infant as and when that is needed, while also encouraging the development of the child's own selfhood and sense of identity.

There is a similar process in supervision and, to a lesser extent, in consultation. In the early stages the learner may be excessively dependent on the supervisor, demanding guidance for every action. The supervisor can be guilty of faulty holding in two ways: On one hand allowing the dependency to continue too long and shielding the student from the experience and the consequences of independent work, on the other hand, expecting the student to undertake too much too soon and exaggerating his anxieties to the extent that he is unable to function at all. The supervisory relationship has to act as a 'container' for the student's anxieties, thus setting him free to give himself to the work in hand, and to establish his own professional identity as a pastor. While the role model presented by the supervisor will affect the style of ministry adopted by the learner, the task for the supervisor is not to produce a carbon copy of himself or herself, but to allow the student to separate himself gradually and to develop his own style of ministry with its own integrity. Supervisor and student are confronted with something of a tightrope to walk in their work together. In this chapter we will explore the problems and possibilities that await them, drawing on the stories of the earlier chapters as examples.

### 'Problems about Learning' and 'Learning Problems'

Someone exercising a ministry of pastoral care under supervision is inevitably involved simultaneously in two separate relationships. There is the relationship with those to whom pastoral care is being offered (the pastor — client axis of the Rhombus theory), and the relationship between the pastor and his supervisor (the supervisor — pastor axis). Each of these relationships presents particular problems for the pastor and the supervisor. Ekstein and Wallerstein draw a useful distinction between these, calling the former 'Learning Problems', and the latter 'Problems about Learning'.[3] The use of the word 'problem' is unfortunate since it suggests that an ideal, problem-free relationship could exist. It is, however, precisely through reflecting on the 'problems', in other words the realities of the relationships and the anxieties engendered within them, that genuine learning takes place.

The problem about learning is not just to be seen as an obstacle on the pathway to increased personal skill; it is rather the very road the student and teacher (consultant and consultee) have undertaken to travel together toward their common goal. In this sense there is always a problem about learning in the most 'normal' of supervisory and consultative interactions.

## Problems about Learning

Every relationship between two people is different and generates issues that are peculiar to it. Problems about Learning refer to those issues which arise between pastor and supervisor in their work together. Although each is again unique, the kind of tensions and difficulties which arise have similarities that can be recognised. These are some of the most common and typical examples.

### 1. *The authority of the supervisor*

At times it is difficult for either the student or the supervisor to accept the authority of the latter. Students can reject the suggestions made, be deaf to the advice which is proffered and in one way or another ignore the experience and expertise of their supervisor. John in his second meeting with his supervisor would not accept the idea that they were beginning to quarrel in a way that might remind him of what he witnessed at home between his parents. Rachel was equally resistant to her supervisor's attempt to show her the effect of her interaction with patients. She took personally the suggestion that she preached at them. Although she clearly offered the patients much more than this, she was so preoccupied with saying the right thing, and so hurt at being criticised, that she missed altogether the positive impact of her behaviour, which her supervisor was keen to reinforce.

Supervisors too can find it difficult to accept their own authority, and can be unsure of what they have to offer. Rachel's supervisor allowed her to slip away prematurely from their first meeting. Gifted and able students will present their work in such a way as to make their supervisors feel redundant. John in the meeting mentioned above arrived full of his success in pastoring the elderly, and implied by his lateness the relative unimportance of supervision now that he had learnt what to do. Peter's resistance of Mary in the consultative triad is an illustration of the same phenomenon, and the one that Paul exploited to help Peter understand what might be happening to him in his work.

### 2. *Dependence upon the supervisor*

The other side of this coin is when students are totally or almost totally dependent upon their supervisors. Students can be so anxious about what they are to do or say that they will do nothing without specific guidance. And they can induce such anxiety in their supervisors that they will do more and more for them. Flattering as it is to have students hanging upon one's every word, this is usually a sign of students' inability to trust their own experience as sufficient basis for learning. Ian after his visit to Mrs Brown might well have been reduced to such feelings of incompetence that he would have accepted quite uncritically any advice from the minister, and would have been even more relieved if the minister had taken over the future visiting of Mrs Brown for him. Students with problems about learning can all too easily hand over their learning and all their work to their supervisors.

### 3. *Evasions of agreed protocol*

Another sign of a problem about learning is when students and supervisors begin to avoid or change their agreed contract. Material for supervision is not produced, appointments are forgotten, or the participants arrive late, as John did for his second meeting with his supervisor. The significance of such changes, which can appear to be of little consequence, is in the effect which they have, and what they reveal both of the actors and of the drama itself. Until that meeting John had been meticulous in his observation of the agreed protocol for supervision. His lateness was out of character, and what is more he was unaware of it. Something hidden to him was happening, and on the surface the only clue was his change in behaviour. The effect this had on the supervisor provided a further clue, and the basis for an idea about the way in which John was responding to his experience of pastoring the elderly. The value of an agreed-upon contract, the structure and boundaries of supervision, is simply that it enables supervisors and students to see when and how the unconscious pressures of the work begin to make their presence felt. Behaviour is like a signpost drawing attention to the problems about learning, of which we would otherwise be ignorant. Initially John would have nothing to do with his supervisor's hypothesis that his behaviour illustrated his inclination to divide people into those worth caring for and those to be ignored, as his parents had done. But a seed is now sown, an idea given, which John need not ignore and which will be confirmed or modified by more experience.

The most common ways in which students and supervisors alter the contract for supervision are either to personalise or intellectualise their work. In the first the focus in supervision will move to the personal needs or problems of the student. Supervision is sufficiently like counselling for this to happen quite naturally. John is a good example of how this might have happened. He offered some very personal facts in his first interview, which could have drawn his supervisor away from his work and into an exploration of his family history. As we saw, the supervisor tried to resist this by relating John's personal experience to the work that was confronting him. At such times a supervisor's experience and expertise as a counsellor can be subtly commissioned and supervision pushed to one side.

Intellectualising problems is another way of avoiding the contract of supervision. Rachel's supervisor was drawn into a discussion about the way Rachel related to patients. She tried again and again to explain what it was Rachel was doing, to teach her in a logical and rational way, but to little effect. Her supervisor was then determined to stop explaining, that is intellectualising, and instead enact the verbatims with Rachel, in the belief that if Rachel experienced her way of talking she would begin to understand its effect. Rachel of course prevented this happening for some time. Her problem about learning emerged through her retreat into intellectualising, and revealed an inability to recognise her considerable emotional and personal gifts as a pastor.

## Games in supervision

The problems about learning which inevitably engage supervisor and student, particularly in the early stages of their work together, are of the utmost importance. They help alert the participants to the anxieties which emerge from the work itself, and which supervision has to contain sufficiently for effective work to be done. They help the aspiring shepherd to recognise both strengths and weaknesses, and how these can be fashioned and modified through the experience itself and reflection upon it. In his important book *Supervision in Social Work*, Kadushin takes up the metaphor of 'games' to describe how the problems about learning are most likely to appear in supervision.[4] Berne, the pioneer of transactional analysis and author of the book *Games People Play*, defines a game as an 'ongoing series of complementary ulterior transactions, superficially plausible, but with a concealed motivation'.[5] Supervision is directed towards a change in behaviour, and such changes are likely to be painful and anxiety-provoking experiences. Games are indulged in as an attempt to reduce anxiety.

The games played by supervisees illustrate, in a light-hearted way, some of the 'Problems about Learning' previously identified. Kadushin's work refers of course to the training of social workers but it may easily be adapted to demonstrate some of the games played by both learners and supervisors in pastoral education. Among the most common of the games played by learners in pastoral education we find:

*I have three papers to write this week.* In this game the learner resists demands to produce a verbatim by pleading that his academic load is excessive. The supervisor should check that the learner is not playing another similar game with his academic tutors, viz. *Don't you know how heavy my field work is?* This pair of games illustrates the need for regular and effective communication between academic teachers and field education supervisors to make sure that one is not being played off against the other.

*You are the best supervisor I have ever had*, in which flattery is used to divert the supervisor from holding the learner to the legitimate agreed task. Most supervisors are vulnerable to the invitation to play this game! The learner may offer expressions of appreciation, such as 'I'll be a better minister because of you', being sensitive to the supervisor's own need to be needed.

In *Treat me, don't beat me*, the learner seeks to change the supervisory relationship into a counselling one. Ministers, who feel themselves 'called to care', may find it hard tò resist this game which in essence allows the learner to expose *himself* rather than his *work*.

*Evaluation is not for friends* also seeks to redefine the supervisory relationship. The learner seeks to befriend the supervisor or establish a social relationship outside the work setting, perhaps so that the supervisor finds it hard to hold his new 'friend' to the agreed task.

The following two games may be offered by the learner as an attempt to reduce a perceived disparity between himself and the supervisor:

*If you knew Tillich like I know Tillich.* In this game a student may display a superior or more up-to-date theological knowledge than the supervisor. Supervisors tend to find this threatening! They may respond by admitting that they have read little of Tillich, leaving themselves in a decidedly 'one-down' position, or else they may refuse to acknowledge their ignorance and work on in the continual fear of having their bluff called. On the other hand, they may know Tillich better than the student and call his bluff!

*What do you know about it anyway?* This game may be played by mature students who perceive themselves as being more experienced than the supervisor in some areas of life, for instance by married students with an unmarried supervisor, by reformed alcoholics, or by older students with wider experience of church life in relation to a young supervisor.

Other games seek to give the learner a greater measure of control in the supervisory relationship:

In *I've got a little list*, the learner comes to a session with a list of questions to ask the supervisor. A question is asked, the supervisor responds and as soon as he shows signs of coming to a stop another question is asked. The learner thus controls both the content and the direction of supervision by appealing to the supervisor's narcissistic gratification in displaying his knowledge.

In *Heading them off at the pass*, the learner openly admits to his poor work so that the supervisor has little alternative but to show sympathy and no genuine supervision takes place.

*I did it like you told me* is an attempt by the learner to blame the supervisor for work which has not turned out right.

*What you don't know won't hurt me.* In this game the learner only presents those aspects of his work which show him in a good light.

It is not, however, only students who play games in supervision, and Kadushin points out some games commonly played by supervisors:

*I wonder why you said that.* This is the game of redefining honest disagreement so that it appears to be psychological resistance. Instead of engaging in a rational discussion based on evidence, the emphasis is shifted to the psychological defences of the student.

*One good question deserves another.* In this game the supervisor asks a learner to work out the answer to his own problem, while the supervisor desperately tries to work it out for herself. If neither comes up with an answer, the supervisor suggests that the learner goes away and thinks about it some more so that they can discuss it next time, and meanwhile the supervisor finds out the answer.

*I can hardly catch my breath.* This is the supervisor's flight from supervision, as he pleads that the demands of the church/hospital mean that he must postpone the supervision session.

Games are only possible when two parties want to play them. A supervisor can prevent games by refusing to play or by confrontation. In refusing to play, the supervisor must be willing to forsake his own advantages, and exercise a self-denying ordinance on the fruits of flattery or of being liked. If a confrontational approach is to be used, it must be done with care, realising the defensive significance of the game for the learner. This is, however, a different way:

> Perhaps another approach is to share honestly with the supervisee one's own awareness of what he is attempting to do but to focus neither on the dynamics of his behaviour nor on one's reaction to it but on the disadvantages for him in playing games. These games have decided drawbacks for the supervisee in that they deny him the possibility of effectively fulfilling one of the essential principal purposes of supervision—helping him grow professionally. The games frustrate the achievement of this outcome. In playing games the supervisee loses by winning.[6]

## Overcoming resistance

In order to treat Problems about Learning constructively, supervisors and their students need to understand something of our natural but unconscious methods of coping, our defences and resistance. Continuing the image of 'holding', we will all protect ourselves against, and hold ourselves away from, anxiety. We need our defences if we are to function at all, and we cannot trust those which are constructed for us, even for our own good, until we have tested them adequately. Thus in supervision students and supervisors have to prove for themselves the process and the reality of the 'holding' which it offers. For students this will mean testing that reality either by protecting themselves and withdrawing from engagement as Rachel, Nigel and Peter did, or by attacking the supervision and supervisor as John did. The supervisor has first to deal with this testing, and await the students' own dismantling or modifying of their defences, and their growing trust in the 'holding' which supervision can provide. David Myler from his long experience of supervising students from religious backgrounds developed a way of handling their resistance. They typically devalued and attacked anything 'psychological', and were more at home with theological and biblical representations of the same truths. Myler draws upon four biblical characters, Adam, Jacob, Moses and the Gerasene demon, to illustrate the kind of games, avoidance and resistance he met in his students. He makes an analogy between the biblical characters' resistance to God's covenant and Jesus' ministry, and students' resistance to their learning contracts. He then goes on to define a theory about the particular problem or anxiety which provokes each kind of resistance, and the most effective strategy for supervisors to use in order to help students overcome their resistance.[7] Here is a flavour of each of the characters and Myler's scheme of supervising them.

He begins by introducing the analogy. 'I suggest that an analogy be drawn between resistance to the learning contract and "sin". I am *not* saying that resistance is actually sinful.'

## Adam

Adam had a variety of reactions to having sinned. He was ashamed, he tried to cover up his nakedness, he blamed others, and he feared losing God's blessing. It could be argued that Adam needed what he resisted . . . the fall. He needed to accept himself as a sinner in order to become human and join the company of the created.

Adam the student also is ashamed of his sin. He resists the learning contract, because it implies that he has something to learn. Adam the student comes in many forms. He or she 'looks' good. He is a high achiever, and presents his best work. Unless otherwise supervised Adam's energies will be focused on avoiding being seen as someone who has something to learn. He is stuck at the *confessional* stage of the salvatory process. He fears confessing because he fears the loss of God's blessing. Adam's fear and shame at being a 'sinner' need to be dealt with gracefully. The supervisor will need to bless him when Adam feels he least deserves it. He will need to help Adam not to reveal his nakedness too quickly. That will cause Adam to hide in the garden, where only God and not the supervisor will find him!

*Jacob*

Isaac's blessing should have been Esau's, but Jacob received it instead. Why? Because Jacob's mother wanted him and not Esau to have it, and Jacob did as his mother wanted. He sought to please his mother. Jacob needed blessing from all those around him, and he did not question whether his behaviour was right or just or genuine. Jacob's only fear was that his deception would be discovered.

The primary need of Jacob the student is to seek blessing . . . approval . . . from all those around him or her. The need to be blessed by others will be sought, even if it takes deception to achieve it (and it does). He will try to please everyone, not just his supervisor. He will be the one who gets into trouble by doing what a nurse or social worker tells him to do, even if it goes against his better judgement. His response to being discovered as 'sinful' will be a quick and easy confession. He will agree with all criticism in order to disarm the process, and restore the approval of all. The more he talks of change the less he seems to change. He is stuck at the *grace* stage of the salvatory process. He does not know who he is. Jacob is whoever he senses others want him to be. There is no sense of self available to receive grace. He needs to turn away from doing what others want, to take off his lambskin and accept himself as a smooth man. Jacob's resistance is difficult to supervise. Esau was a hairy man, but Jacob is a slippery one. The supervisor needs to provide strict limits, clear contracting and firm faithfulness. Jacob needs external help to see the way in which his need to be approved supersedes all else. The supervisor will need to maintain distance and avoid friendship with Jacob, which is difficult because Jacob is usually very likeable. Too much distance by the supervisor can be overwhelming for Jacob and lead to panic or withdrawal.

## Moses

Moses is someone who really had some resistance to a covenant. In spite of his royal upbringing and superior education, he resisted God's call. He admitted his sinfulness as a way of avoiding responsibility for his life. He put himself down as someone unfit to approach Pharoah. He was not eloquent enough, others could do a better job, people would not accept him—the list could go on because Moses resisted God's covenant for chapters!

Moses the student can resist as well. He or she has not got what it takes to fulfil a learning contract. When pushed he will freely discuss the 'sinfulness' which prevents him from doing better. Moses will only share verbatims which exhibit this 'sinfulness'. The supervisor will want to help poor helpless Moses, and much time will be spent reaching out to help him. Moses will be given the right words to say, the pastoral skills to use, but like the biblical Moses will continue to resist. Moses is stuck at the *repentance* stage. He argues that he is unable to repent, he is too inadequate to change and grow. His confessions need to be discouraged, and the focus put upon his strength and ability to fulfil the learning contract. The message to him is 'In spite of your sinfulness, which really is no greater than that of most others, you have the strength to repent, to learn; however only *you* can repent'. The supervisor must try to avoid rescuing Moses; such rescuing only reinforces the message that Moses is too incompetent.

## The Gerasene Demoniac

The Gerasene's reaction to sin is to be wildly out of control, self-destructive and resistant to salvation. He frightened those around him and was expelled. He was, however, a strong person, he broke his chains, and he was the only one who recognised Jesus as the Christ.

The student Gerasene's reaction to the learning contract is to be out of control, to overreact, and to resist help. He or she can rage at criticism, and weep tears of helplessness, and will be without limits in terms of emotionality and behaviour. He is capable of embarrassing the supervisor by his performances.

He is stuck at the *forgiveness* stage of the salvatory process. He not only needs forgiveness but a form of forgiveness which is externally focused; he needs to hear from someone in authority that he is forgiven. This helps him get his 'sin' reaction under control. The supervisor needs to avoid joining in a focus on the out-of-control behaviour. He needs to set limits to the unacceptable behaviour and to keep them. He should not be tempted to abandon a professional focus in supervision and to turn to therapy issues.

Myler concludes that he 'has found dramatic change in the Gerasene to be trustworthy, but that his peer group may resist helpful changes in the student Gerasene, because his out-of-control behaviour provided a good deal of agenda and effect'.[8]

This Summary Chart illustrates the essential parts of each character:

## SUMMARY CHART

| TYPOLOGY | REACTION TO 'SIN' | FOCUS WITHIN SALVATORY PROCESS | SUPERVISORY INTERVENTIONS |
|---|---|---|---|
| ADAM | + Blameless<br>+ Shame/ Embarrassment<br>+ Hiddenness<br>+ Fear of God's curse | CONFESSION: Ashamed to confess that he is a sinner | + Communicate care and acceptance<br>+ Withhold blessing for 'good works'<br>+ Keep some distance and tension in relationship<br>+ Bless him when he 'confesses' and feels least worthy of blessing |
| JACOB | + Easy convert<br>+ Shame<br>+ Deception<br>+ Fear of everyone's curse | GRACE: Difficulty accepting grace because he has lost any sense of self | + Bless when honest and in touch with self<br>+ Distrust quick changes<br>+ 'Name the Game'<br>+ Strict adherence to learning contract |

| MOSES | + Helpless<br>+ Sin is a way<br>to avoid<br>responsibility<br>for change<br>+ Confesses<br>easily | REPENTANCE:<br>Resists changing<br>'sinful' behaviour | + Set limits on<br>amount of 'confess-<br>ing' tolerated<br>+ Emphasise his/her<br>strength<br>+ Encourage self-<br>initiative and<br>responsibility<br>+ Resist 'rescuing'<br>+ Strict adherence<br>to learning contract |
| GERASENE | + Goes out of<br>control<br>+ All is crisis<br>+ Loss of limits<br>+ Fear/Anger<br>+ Acts out | FORGIVENESS:<br>Needs to hear<br>firm, unam-<br>biguous word of<br>forgiveness from<br>someone in<br>authority | + Avoid focus on<br>crisis behaviour<br>+ Firm limits viz.<br>behaviour, super-<br>visory time, learning<br>contract<br>+ Avoid focus on<br>therapy issues<br>+ Affirm that<br>student can/will<br>tolerate limits<br>+ Dramatic changes<br>more trustworthy<br>+ Supervise peer<br>group resistance to<br>Gerasene's changes |

## Learning Problems

Just as every supervisory relationship is unique, so every pastoral relationship has its own particular issues. The phrase 'Learning Problems' is used to designate those issues and problems which arise when a learner begins to be involved in the practice of pastoral care and relationships with those who are to be cared for (the pastor—client axis of the Rhombus). Among the most common are these:

### 1. *The preacher*

Students coming directly from college and lay people whose own faith and confidence is relatively new, are likely to fall back upon the 'truths' they have received, and rely on other people's wisdom and words. Rather than offer themselves, they will present what the Bible says, or their Church believes, irrespective of the effect it has upon their clients. Rachel was inclined to do this when faced with the sufferings of the patients. She wanted her faith to be some help to them, and using her teaching skills she tried to force her message home.

## 2. The non-directive counsellor

This is the opposite of the stance outlined above. It may stem either from extreme passivity in the learner, or an inappropriate application of the client-centred approach of Carl Rogers. The effect is to keep the student at a very safe distance from the client, while giving the opposite impression. This caricature of non-directive counselling allows the student to make the minimum contribution, and to hand over the structure of the pastoral relationship entirely to the person seeking help. This leads of course to great frustrations for the client and no development for the student. Students who are genuinely afraid of what they might do or say, and of its damaging effect, are most likely to adopt this way of relating.

## 3. 'Depend on me'

Students are nearly always anxious to be useful and helpful, and so respond very warmly to anyone who appears to need them. We saw how John became very involved with one patient, and then began to notice how much attention that man received from everyone else. In pastoral ministry we will constantly encounter people whose self-esteem is very low, and who cannot or will not decide or do anything for themselves. While it is important for us to be available to people, it is also likely that we will make ourselves so available that we are overwhelmed.

The situation is almost an inevitable trap. The more willing a person is to meet desperate need, the more the needs mount. The greater the demands the less he can do to meet them because his limited resources are spread too thin. This is a problem which besets the pastor more acutely than almost any other professional because he has no clearly defined boundaries to the extent of his professional care.[9]

John's supervisor aimed to help prepare John for this by using the experience of his lateness as a potent example of what he will have to contend with throughout his ministry.

### 4. The compulsive helper

This of course is closely related to the issue above. However, here the problem has its roots not in the dependency needs of the person seeking help, but in the needs of the one offering help. All too often each finds the other and becomes embedded in an unholy alliance. The need to be needed exists in most of us, and can lead us to go many extra and quite unhelpful miles with others. We give away what is of little help to others, and what we really need for ourselves. This need may also manifest itself in an unwillingness to delegate anything to anyone else. Reg wanted to do this but also feared the consequences particularly for his protégée Helen.

### 5. The professor

One way of managing the intense feelings which begin to emerge in a relationship is to talk about them, to keep a safe distance from them by intellectualising and theorising. Had Ian been equipped with some theories on grief he might well have used them to protect himself from Mrs Brown's sudden outburst. Rachel, as we saw, was inclined to begin teaching about the faith when the patients started to introduce their feelings of madness and despair.

Learning problems such as these all provide a positive indication that something of significance is beginning to take place. Usually it means that pastor and pastored have begun to engage, and the emotional weight of the one is passing to the other in order to be shared. At this point it is easy for one or other to take flight. The point of flight is especially important. If it can be recalled during supervision, the precipitating events and feelings can be uncovered. This in turn will lead to the issue or need behind the problem. The feelings are often of the most primitive and extreme kind: sexual intimacy, fear and despair, anger and rage, doubt and judgement, grief and loss, guilt and suicide. Nigel's defence against the latter is well illustrated in the beginning of his conversation with his vicar.

## The parallel process

It is not uncommon to discover that issues which come into prominence in a supervisory relationship (the pastor — supervisor axis of the Rhombus) are similar to the issues that have been important in the pastoral relationship (the pastor — client axis of the Rhombus). This phenomenon, which has been named the 'Parallel Process', has sometimes been described as if it were surprising or coincidental.

> This parallel process carries with it a never ending surprise element as if we should not expect things to turn out as they usually do, as if the occurrence of such parallels is chance, rather than the rule.[10]

On closer consideration, however, it will become evident that these phenomena should not be considered either coincidental or surprising, for both the supervisory relationship and the pastoral relationship have a common factor in the personality of the care-giver.

This phenomenon as an integral part of social work education has been fully discussed by Janet Mattison in her book, *The Reflection Process in Casework Supervision*.[11] 'The thesis is simple', she writes in her introduction, 'the processes at work in the relationship between client and worker are often reflected in the relationship between worker and supervisor.' It must be stressed that the matters under discussion refer to the *normal* relationships between supervisor, learner and person being helped, and not necessarily to any pathological processes. It is not implied that if the learner was really mature, and free from hang-ups, there would be no learning problems, no problems about learning and no parallel process phenomena. These exist not because people are sick but because they are human.

Nevertheless, an awareness of the dynamics of the

relationship between supervisor and learner will often provide insight into how the learner functions in ministry. This was apparent in both John's and Rachel's relationships with their supervisors, and as we saw it was eventually used to good effect. In the same way Paul used his observation of Mary and Peter's relationship as evidence of something that was happening between Peter and the Smith family.

The importance of this phenomenon for supervision is that if the supervisor becomes aware of the dynamics of the supervisory relationship, some clue may be gleaned concerning the crucial factors operative in the pastoral relationship. If the learner has difficulties in coping with the expression of strong feeling in supervision, it is likely that he will avoid strong emotions in his pastoral relationship; if the supervisor becomes aware of issues relating to sexuality or hostility in the supervisory relationship, the learner is probably experiencing difficulties in these areas of his pastoral work; if the learner seems anxious to please the supervisor, he is also probably anxious to please the person he is trying to help. In short, the presence of a 'Problem about Learning' in the supervisory relationship may provide a valuable clue to the 'Learning Problems' which exist in pastoral relationships.

What is more, supervisors, by reflecting upon their reactions to those they supervise and the work they hear about, will often become aware of something for which there is no apparent evidence: feelings of anger or boredom, flights of fancy, thoughts and associations. If they can bring these forward and include them in some way, it is likely that they will reveal some of the issues just beneath the surface. We have often used such clues to invite our students to imagine their own words as coming from the mouths of their clients, and then to hear what they sound like.

It is important to recognise that the 'Parallel Process' works both ways, and that what happens between supervisor and student will also be reflected in the relationship between students and their clients. That is why it is so important to spend time in supervision on the supervisory relationship itself. So that whatever is happening can be brought into the open and its effects absorbed. In practice this will free students to be more themselves in their work, and to use, rather than be dominated by, their supervisors' experience and expertise. Supervisors are also helped in this if they take time to share their work with colleagues.

The nature of the 'holding' of supervision, the management of both Learning Problems and Problems about Learning, and the Parallel Process can be seen diagramatically as follows:

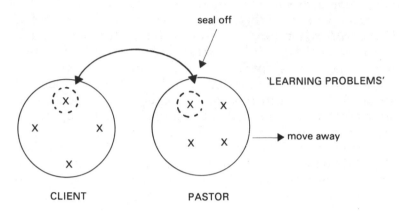

The client shares his story with his pastor; as he does so he begins to convey feelings as well as facts. His 'wounds' (x) begin to show and are felt like echoes that resound within the pastor, who will have felt similar feelings and may indeed have similar 'wounds' (x). In order to protect herself from the 'hurt' of those 'wounds' the pastor has to defend herself against the client. Her 'Learning Problems' are the signs of her defence. Some will seal her off, making her impervious to the client's 'hurt'; others will distance her from him so that the echoes die of their own accord (Nigel appeared to be doing this in relation to Evelyn). The supervisor aims to help her contain more and more of what her client shares, and to manage the cost of it to herself more effectively. Because she cannot at once trust him and his supervision she will have to resist him as well, hence her 'Problems about Learning'.

The 'holding' of supervision is achieved when a space is created within the pastor, which enables her to separate her personal and professional identity in such a way that feelings and thoughts can flow between those identities but that she has some control over the currents. In other words, there is a 'semi-permeable membrane' between the 'person' and the 'pastor' within her, as there is between her and her client and her and her supervisor. Supervision can then be focused on the work that she can do for the client in that space by thinking and feeling from within herself, and then offered back to the client in the form of a response or an interpretation. The supervisor's task is to watch over and care for both the work and the membranes that hold and contain it.

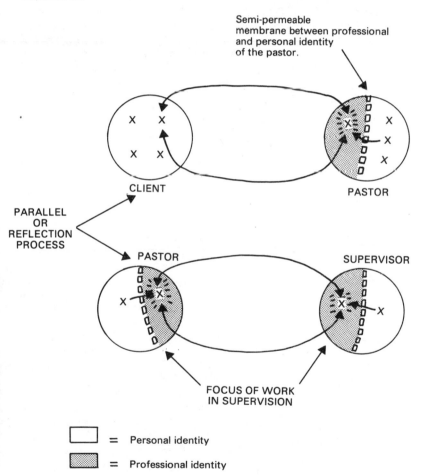

Semi-permeable membrane between professional and personal identity of the pastor.

CLIENT

PASTOR

PARALLEL OR REFLECTION PROCESS

PASTOR

SUPERVISOR

FOCUS OF WORK IN SUPERVISION

☐ = Personal identity

▨ = Professional identity

## Notes

1. John 10.1–18.
2. Winnicott, D. W., *The Family and Individual Development*, Tavistock 1965, p. 18.
3. Ekstein, R., and Wallerstein, R. S., *The Teaching and Learning of Psychotherapy*, 2nd edn, New York: International Universities Press 1972.
4. Kadushin, A., *Supervision in Social Work,* New York: Columbia University Press, 1976.
5. Berne, E., *Games People Play*, André Deutsch 1966, p. 48.
6. Kadushin, A., 'Games People Play in Social Work', *Social Work* 13, 1968, p. 32.
7. Myler, D., 'Resistance to Clinical Learning: Four Biblical Types', *Journal of Supervision and Training in Ministry*, Chicago, vol 2, 1979, pp. 73–81.
8. Myler, op. cit., p. 81.
9. Anon., 'Pastoral Availability' *Contact* 15, Oct 1965, p. 9.
10. Ekstein and Wallerstein, op. cit., p. 177.
11. Mattison, J., *The Reflection Process in Casework Supervision*, Institute of Marital Studies, 1975, p. 11.

NINE

# The Practicalities of Learning

In this final chapter we will describe some of the essential and practical aspects of supervision and then of consultation. Much of this was implicit in the earlier chapters, to which we will continue to refer.

Before either supervision or consultation can take place, the pastoral care to be supervised or consulted about has to be practised or at least planned. Both are therefore determined in part by the context and the activities which are the focus of the student's or colleague's work and practice. For some it will be a matter of receiving supervision for the whole of their ministry. This is the case for newly ordained and licensed pastors like Nigel in Chapter 4. For others supervision will be part of some specific experience within their training, as in the case of students sent to practise pastoral care in parishes and institutions. And for others supervision will focus on a particular aspect of care, or a role for which they are training, as was the case with Reg's bereavement counsellors in Chapter 6. For the purpose of this chapter we will use the term 'placement' to refer to all these different foci.

## THE PRACTICALITIES OF SUPERVISION

In all the stories and situations already illustrated it is clear that any opportunity for pastors to learn from their experience and practice involves a number of people, parties and agencies. It is important that all these play a part in establishing a placement. There will normally be four different parties to any placement:

1 The student or worker coming on the placement;
2 The supervisor responsible for their work and learning in the placement;

3 The institution or training authority responsible for the student;
4 The institution, parish, hospital, community etc. to which the student comes.

All should be consulted prior to the placement beginning and the needs and expectations of each elicited and communicated to the others. The supervisor (2) and the training institution (3) are best placed to see that this is done and that the objectives of the placement are understood by all concerned. An example of this appears in Chapter 5 with Rachel's placement in a psychiatric hospital. Once the placement is established then a Learning Agreement or Contract can be drawn up by the student and the supervisor.

### The Learning Agreement

This may be defined as 'a written document, which should be drawn up by the student and agreed with the supervisor, which embodies the objectives for the placement and the means by which the objectives are to be met.' These can be listed first as specific goals and then extended to include the stages and methods by which the student plans to achieve the goals. John in Chapter 3 wanted to learn about working with the elderly. As we saw, this entailed a number of elements:

1 Actual experience of visiting elderly people in hospital;
2 The opportunity to see how other professions cared for them;
3 Exploration of his own experience of the elderly in his family;
4 Reading about the experiences of the elderly themselves;
5 The supervision he received, which helped him to integrate all the above.

Some of these elements would have been clear at the beginning of the placement; others emerged later and could be added to the Learning Agreement along the way. It is also useful to include in the Agreement, with each of the goals, something about how the student and supervisor plan to assess the student's achievements during, and at the end of, the placement (see Appendix A).

## The Introduction to Supervision

What happens when the door is shut, when supervisor and learner(s) meet together during the time which they have agreed to set aside for supervision? The primary aim of the first one or two supervision sessions must be to establish a good working relationship based on mutual trust. This may involve a fairly open sharing of goals and aspirations on the part of both supervisor and learner, which are brought together in the Learning Agreement. The aim is to build up mutual confidence and trust between two people engaged for a time in a common task of ministry and learning.

This introductory phase will also include a period of orientation, both formal and informal. Formally, the learner needs to know something of the history and geography of the institution in which the placement is set; informally, there is a subtle communication of the style and ethos both of the institution and of the ministry which is related to it.

Once the ground rules have been established and a measure of trust built up, the pattern of a typical supervision session will begin to emerge. The centrepiece may be the discussion of a verbatim prepared by the student. It is a mistake however to proceed to this directly. It is always valuable to provide time at the start of the session for the learners to talk about any matters of pressing concern. A simple question such as 'How have things been going?' will allow an issue to be aired, which has arisen since the verbatim was written, or which was too difficult (or apparently trivial) to write about in a verbatim. This, rather than the material prepared for discussion, may be the royal road to an exploration of issues which are central to the development of the learner's pastoral identity. Valuable as the open discussion at the beginning of a supervision session may be, one must guard against it being abused as a distraction from the central supervisory issues (see Chapter 8 — Games People Play in Supervision — 'I've got a little list').

It is not uncommon in the early stages of a placement for learners to express a degree of disillusionment. They expected to be 'doing counselling' and instead they find themselves in ordinary conversations with ordinary people, who do not

appear to have any problems. The supervisor may be tempted
to give a mini-lecture on the differences between pastoral care
and pastoral counselling. Rather, the learners should be
enabled to reflect on the conversations in which they have
actually been involved, and helped to identify themes of
pastoral significance, or to consider the effect on them of
having had no significant conversations, or of being ignored,
bored and frustrated.

Before students embark on the analysis of a verbatim
produced by one of their own number it may be helpful to
discuss a verbatim of a conversation in which they have not
been personally involved, perhaps one of those in this book.
In his *Pastoral Care in the Modern Hospital* Heije Faber
provides an appendix containing two verbatims and in
*Meaning in Madness* by John Foskett there are a number of
verbatims, which may be used in this way.[1] The advantages
of such a procedure are that the learners see what a typical
verbatim looks like, and at the same time gain a preliminary
appreciation of the learning potential of verbatim analysis
without experiencing any personal threat. The disadvantage
is that they may be unduly influenced by one particular
approach to the writing of verbatims.

There are in fact a number of ways in which learners may
present work to supervisors, of which the use of written
verbatims is only one. We now turn to a detailed consideration
of these.

### The 'Raw Data' of Supervision

There are at least four ways in which learners may bring their
work for supervision: verbal reports by the learner, written
reports by the learner, direct observation of the learner, and
electronic recording.

### *Verbal reports by the learner*

The simplest access to what went on in a pastoral
conversation is the direct report of the person involved. We
shall turn shortly to the use of written reports, especially
verbatims prepared by the learner. While these are important,
and some would claim normative, there is a danger in asking

learners to write reports too soon. In the initial stages of pastoral education the learner is usually fully occupied just in learning to make relationships. To expect a learner to produce a written report of one pastoral conversation, before becoming comfortable in making relationships, is to impose an additional and unnecessary stress. Instead of concentrating on building up relationships, the student will have at the back of his or her mind the need to 'produce a verbatim', so that the first time a conversation moves beyond the superficial, he or she will be trying desperately to remember what went on in order to write it up!

The solution in the early stages of a placement may be to ask the student 'How did you get on?', and then to listen while the story is told. It is sometimes helpful to do this immediately the student returns from an assignment while its emotional impact is still fresh. The student may need to talk briefly at this point either to share any strong feelings which have been aroused, or to express disappointment that 'nothing very much happened'. This method is illustrated by Ian in Chapter 2 who came to his supervisor to talk about his bereavement visit to Mrs Brown. Ian had strong feelings after that visit and as Hamish allowed him to talk about what had happened during the visit, he was able to reflect upon it and learn from the experience.

### Written reports by the learner

A major contribution of the clinical training movement to pastoral education has been its emphasis upon the value of written accounts of actual pastoral encounters. Their introduction is generally attributed to the Rev Russell R. Dicks:

> I was seeing so many different patients . . . that I found it necessary to keep some kind of record. But what kinds of records could I keep? I asked myself what happens when I see a patient? The answer was: we talk. Then what do we say? I began to write down all I could remember of the conversations I had with patients.[2]

Such written accounts of pastoral conversations known as 'verbatims' have come to be of considerable importance in pastoral education and have been used extensively in this book.

A verbatim is the learner's own recollection of what went on in the pastoral education, and usually has three parts:

A. *Introduction* in which the learner states what he knew about the person being visited before the conversation began. This will include details of how the visit came about, information received and observations made.

B. *The record of the conversation* where the learner writes down the process of the conversation as far as it can be remembered. The contributions of the visitor and person being visited are numbered consecutively. It is also useful to record the actions and movements of those involved (like stage directions) and any significant feelings which are not obvious from the words of the conversation.

Thus   M = Minister (student, learner)
        P = Person visited (patient, parishioner).

M1: Hello, Mrs White. I am the new assistant minister at St Mark's Church. May I come in?
P1: Good afternoon. The minister said you would call. Do come in. (*I entered the living room and sat in the chair opposite Mrs White.*)
M2: I was sorry to hear about your mother's death.
P2: Yes, but it was very peaceful . . .

*Evaluation* in which the student considers a number of relevant questions about the conversation, e.g. What was going on? What (if anything) did the person expect from me? Did I understand the feelings expressed? What might I have done differently? What can I learn from this conversation about the way in which I function as a pastor.

The learner should be encouraged to write up the conversation as soon as possible after the visit, or at least to jot down key words and phrases so that the conversation can be written down later.

A verbatim will never be the same as the transcript of an electronic recording of a conversation. It is not meant to be. It is the learner's recollection of what went on and is necessarily subjective and selective. This does not detract from its value as a learning tool, for the learner's *perception* of what went on in the visit is as important (perhaps even more important) as the 'bare facts' of the event. This is the raw data of supervision (blank forms for the writing up of verbatims are shown in Appendix B).

While verbatims have been the most commonly used means of reporting in pastoral education, other methods are also possible. More common in social work training, *Process Reports*, which are written accounts of what transpires in a situation over a period of time, may be a useful tool. These differ from *Case Studies* in that the former are written up consecutively as a situation develops, while the latter are written up at the conclusion of a period of significant involvement in a situation. It is also possible to ask a student to prepare a *critical incident report*, i.e. a written and detailed account of what transpired in one particular act of ministry which had special significance (either positive or negative) for the student. Keeping a *Diary* or *Journal* may also be a significant way of recording what went on in a placement. It is important, however, that the diary should be more than a record of events, and include the learner's attempts to record his feelings about these events, and to reflect theologically on them.

Eventually a student will produce a verbatim. How can it best be used? There are two possible approaches:

(a) The supervisor receives it before the time arranged for supervision. This gives time for the supervisor to read it and decide on the most important issues to raise. We saw an example of this approach in Rachel's second verbatim. This, however, may lead to a didactic approach on the part of the supervisor, as when an essay has been handed in to a tutor. It also tends to be less interactive than the second approach to which we now turn.

(b) The student brings the verbatim to the actual supervision session, and the supervisor and learner read it together. The learner can then relate to the verbatim in one of two ways. He can read his own part and hear himself again, perhaps perceiving that the conversation did not go as badly as he thought. This was the approach used by Rachel's supervisor in the third verbatim; it was initially resisted by Rachel, although in the long run, the exploration of Rachel's resistance turned out to be very productive in helping her understand how she related to people. Alternatively, the learner may read the part of the patient or parishioner and the supervisor that of the learner. This helps the learner to 'get inside the skin' of the patient, and hear his or her own words coming from the lips of the supervisor. This interchange of roles can help both learner and supervisor experience some of the dynamics of the interview in a fresh way. It also leads to a more lively and interactive supervisory process.

If the verbatim is used in a group, then the student presenting the verbatim may be excluded from the reading, and asked to remain silent for the time being, while others take the parts in the verbatim. It may well be that the other students will ask some pertinent questions which will enable the one presenting the case to reflect on the practice of ministry. What did it feel like to hear someone else reading your words? Did your feelings change as the reading proceeded? Would you now wish to say or do anything different at any point? What feelings or reflections are you left with now that the reading is over?

## Direct observation of the learner

This is only possible to a limited degree. If the 'raw data' of supervision is the learner's conduct of worship or the preaching of a sermon, then obviously the minister/supervisor has direct access to what will be on the agenda for the supervisory meeting. When, however, the act of ministry is a less public one, such as a visit to a bereaved family, then direct observation of the learner is just not possible. Even when it is possible, there is the problem that direct observation may affect the performance of the learner, and may generate feelings of not being trusted or even of persecution.

It is worth noting in passing that while direct observation of the learner's *ministry* may not be possible, direct observation in other settings, such as in the supervision group, will often reveal much of a student's style and method.

*Electronic recording*

To overcome the problem of a lack of direct observation, it has been suggested that audio- and/or video-recordings could be used to bring the 'truth' of the pastoral encounter into the supervisory conference. It is a method which has been used in the training of secular counsellors. There are, however, considerable problems. The conversations of pastors occur in many places where access to this machinery is not possible or appropriate. Further, if the learners know they are being taped, they may well be much more hesitant in their responses, seeking to model themselves on what they *think* is the right approach, or on their supervisor, rather than working spontaneously or according to their usual pattern.

Nevertheless, video- and audio-recordings of role plays can be most helpful in training. Students can role-play typical interactions and watch and listen to how they come across. Some training schemes use actors for this purpose.

## Confidentiality in supervision

One final point must be made in relation to the discussion of case material, and this relates to the issue of confidentiality. The basic rule, which must be emphasised to learners at the outset of a placement, is that they are bound by the same rules as other professional people and students working within an institution, be it a hospital, congregation, or any other. The details of other people's lives must not be discussed beyond the professional setting. When patients or parishioners are discussed in supervision, as in a verbatim, they may be given fictitious names or identified by a letter (Mr A, Mrs B etc).

Nevertheless, while the basic rule stands, the situation in practice may be more subtle and complex. In undertaking a hospital placement, the student may participate in team meetings at which details of the private lives of patients are discussed. The student must be enabled to develop the professional judgement which helps him or her share such information without divulging what was said under the seal of pastoral confidentiality. This is never an easy decision, and while there is a 'corporate confidentiality' shared collectively by the team as well as individual confidentiality, wherever possible the patient should know that this happens and be assured that this sharing of information is in his or her own interests.

Further, in a parish setting, it will sometimes happen that minister and assistant are sharing the pastoral care of a family or individual. It will be virtually impossible to reflect upon their joint ministry without discussing their individual understandings of what is happening in a given situation. There may even be situations when a parishioner attempts to play off one carer against the other. Those who engage in pastoral ministry will be wise not to be flattered by such statements as 'You are the only person who really understands me. I can't talk to the vicar/curate the way I talk to you.' There must be trust and at least a limited sharing of confidences within the team, but a sharing which does not go beyond the team.

### The evaluation of the Placement

If the clarification of goals is one element in a successful placement, another is its proper evaluation. The subject of evaluation is one which is notoriously difficult and relatively unexplored, and it is probable that these two facts are not unrelated. The complexity derives, in part, from the fact that the placement is inevitably viewed from different perspectives by the various parties to the placement. The college will want to know if it provided good learning opportunities for the student: 'Do we want to send someone there next year?' The minister and the congregation will make their own evaluation: 'It was good to have her with us. She worked hard, got involved, gave of herself. We would like another student'.

This kind of evaluation is important and takes its own course. Our primary focus at this point, however, must be on a particular kind of evaluation. Has the student's performance been of a sufficiently high standard to allow him or her to proceed to the next career stage? This is never an easy question to answer. How does one evaluate pastoral practice? It is difficult enough to evaluate a piece of written work such as an essay, for even this comparatively easy exercise can produce a variety of judgements from different markers. How much more difficult, then, to evaluate not a report describing some act of pastoral ministry, but the act itself. Sometimes the failure lies in a failure to identify the objective of the evaluation exercise. Is it to pass judgement on the activities of the learner or to facilitate the learning process itself? Inevitably some forms of evaluation must have an element of judgement in them. If a parish placement is a required component of a course of preparation for ministry, then the college or sponsoring church committee will want to be assured that the student has attained a satisfactory standard of ministerial practice. If a hospital placement is an integral part of a course on pastoral care and counselling, then a student who scored high marks in an examination on counselling theory, but who had learnt nothing about relating to people, could not be passed.

Evaluation in pastoral education should, however, have a deeper purpose than simply to pass judgement upon performance. Evaluation should enable a learner to con-solidate and internalise the insights gained in the placement. We are in fact identifying two different approaches to evaluation. A book on the training of general practitioners has labelled these *summative* evaluation, which occurs at the conclusion of a course of study, and *formative* evaluation, which is integral to the learning process itself.[3] Ideally, the evaluation of pastoral education will be of the formative rather than the summative type.

Part of each meeting for supervision will have an evaluative component. In addition it is often helpful to have a *midpoint evaluation* halfway through the expected duration of a placement, so that insights gained can be acknowledged and objectives for the second half of the placement adjusted if necessary.

The kind of evaluation which contributes to the total learning experience will take place through open communic-ation between the parties involved in the placement. The Learning Agreement negotiated at the beginning of the placement may form a convenient starting point for this discussion, embodying as it does mutually agreed objectives. The basic question is, 'To what extent have these objectives been achieved?' This question will be addressed both at the midway evaluation and in the final phase of supervision when supervisor and learner are reflecting together on the course of the placement. But other voices need to be heard as well. If there has been an active group of lay people supporting the learner during the placement, the members of that group may have insightful comments to make and these can best be expressed in a setting which is at the same time structured and relaxed. If the learner has been one of a group of students, the final meetings of that will provide valuable insights for each of the members. And if the learner has been part of a multidisciplinary team, the members of the team will have their reactions to contribute.

Ultimately, however, the final evaluation will probably take the form of a written report in which both supervisor and learner have a hand, drawing on the insights of the others where appropriate. The student may be asked to complete an Evaluation Form such as that shown in Appendix C. This has been used in hospital placements and asks students to identify their strengths and weaknesses as pastors in relation to patients, staff, other students, the supervisor, themselves and God. The supervisor writes his assessment under the same categories, with input from the peer group, and eventually a combined report is produced. Clearly, since the learner has been involved in continuous assessment throughout the placement, the report will contain few surprises. Indeed a major focus of the report will be the way in which the learner has responded to the feedback which he or she has been receiving and the extent to which he or she has 'learnt how to learn'. While the report may not express unanimity on all points, it will expose areas of agreement and disagreement, and hopefully will identify areas uncovered for future learning by the student.

We are now in a position to examine the factors which contribute to personal and professional growth in a placement.

### Placement Criteria

What makes a good placement? If we cannot accept the premise that a learner can simply be dropped into a situation and automatically benefit from the experience, what factors are essential, or at least desirable, for optimum learning?

Four such criteria may be identified, with the first two, at least, coming into the essential category: (a) a setting which provides realistic tasks for the learner; (b) a setting which provides supervision by a qualified supervisor actively involved in ministry within that setting; (c) a setting with an interdisciplinary dimension; (d) a setting where there is more than one learner.

*A setting which provides realistic tasks for the learner*

The examples earlier in this book illustrate the importance of matching the students to the placement and vice versa. This means setting reasonable limits to the number and scale of activities in which students are involved. It is best to restrict the students' experience to a manageable number of relationships with individuals and groups so as to allow as much time within the placement for observation and reflection as for action and involvement. The specific tasks allotted to students should be appropriate to their own learning goals and their level of competence and experience.

*A setting which provides supervision by a qualified supervisor who is actively involved in ministry within that setting*

Supervision should be provided by persons who are an integral part of the setting of the placement, such as the minister or priest in a parish placement, or the chaplain in an institutional one. Ideally these persons should be trained and qualified as supervisors in addition to their own professional training as pastors. The Association for Pastoral Care and Counselling does accredit supervisors, and a number of institutions provide training courses in supervision.[4] If these resources are not available it is important that all supervisors receive some training and support for their work. The training institutions from which the students come or the denominational training bodies are the most obvious resources for this. Alternatively, supervisors themselves can provide some mutual support and training for one another.

If the two factors identified above may be considered essential for a good placement, a further two may be deemed desirable.

## A setting with an interdisciplinary dimension

This is probably more practicable in institutional settings than in local congregations. There is, however, great value in helping learners relate to members of different professions and others in the body of Christ. Not only do pastoral care students gain an understanding of other disciplines, they also begin to work out their own role in relation to them and, in a parochial setting, to the other pastors within the congregation.

## A setting in which there is more than one learner

A major strength of the clinical pastoral education movement has been the peer group experience, where interaction within the group provides a vehicle for personal learning. Sometimes only one student or assistant is attached to a congregation, and it can be difficult, if not impossible, to arrange this within a parish setting. Steps should be taken, however, to provide another group setting in which there can be some experience of shared reflection on the practice of ministry. Theological colleges should find it possible to provide this experience for their students, and those responsible for the further education of assistant ministers and curates should be able to provide a structure in which this can take place, such as pastoral training and support groups referred to later in this chapter.

Wherein lies the value of the peer group experience? First, at the most basic level there can be a sharing of experience. Women and men in their first forays into ministry can compare notes and find that they are not alone in their uncertainties and anxieties. Secondly, as the learner describes some aspect of work there can be both challenge and support. Both are needed. Sometimes a learner will need to hear the questions of peers regarding methods, motives and theological presuppositions relating to a particular piece of ministry; sometimes support and encouragement will be forthcoming. Finally, in a group setting a learner will have conveyed an impression of how he or she comes across as a person and a minister. Once trust has been established, the group becomes a 'safe' place where, in a supportive environment, a learner is able to hear the sometimes hard words of personal truth.

The presence of a supervisor, or some other kind of consultant or group facilitator, may provide this safe structure where the anxieties generated can be contained. In practice, learners at least initially, or until a degree of trust has been established, may find it more difficult to be open in the group than in private with the supervisor. The result may be that the members of the group engage in a mutually collusive game of 'safety first'.

## Types of Placements

The different settings which can play a significant role in pastoral education may be classified in three ways: (a) In-role and out-of-role placements; (b) Block and concurrent placements; (c) Parochial and non-parochial placements.

### In-role and out-of-role placements

The distinctive feature of an in-role placement is that the learner is clearly perceived as participating in ministry, e.g. as a curate or assistant in a parish, or as a theological student undertaking a placement with a chaplain in a hospital or prison or as a lay visitor. To be labelled 'minister' or 'chaplain' (literally or metaphorically) is to take on at least some of the role expectations of ministry. The main advantage of an in-role placement is that it enables the learner to taste the flavour of 'what it is like' to be a minister without all the pressures and responsibilities of the office. A contribution is made to the professional socialisation of the learner. A parallel phenomenon may be observed in other forms of professional education. From the first moment a medical student dons a white coat and walks into a ward there is a gradual and controlled progression towards the full responsibility of being a doctor.

There may however be an over-rapid assumption of the professional role. This is particularly true in the case of pastoral care where a learner may adopt a stereotype of ministry which is never adequately questioned. Herein lies the value of the out-of-role placement. This may involve a theological student working as an unqualified member of a social work or community development team, or as a nursing auxiliary in a hospital. Such placements have several advantages; the learner acquires some understanding of the world in which ministry must be exercised (particularly important for a theological student who has gone straight from school to university and/or theological college), and does so from the perspective of a group which does not share the assumptions of 'the ministry'. Also there is great value in 'seeing ourselves as others see us'. Finally, out-of-role placements have the advantage of awakening some understanding of the ethos and standards of other professions and groups.

## Block and concurrent placements

In a block placement the learner is engaged full-time for a limited period in the work of the placement. This might be as a probationer minister or curate, once academic requirements are completed, spending a period of time as an assistant in a parish; or, as is common in the United States, a student spending an 'intern year' in a congregation before returning to seminary for a final phase of academic study; or as a student working with a hospital chaplain for six to twelve weeks; or in industrial mission during the summer vacation.

In a concurrent placement, the learner is engaged simultaneously in both academic study and, on a part-time basis, in the work of the placement. For example a student is attached to a congregation for several weeks during the academic year, or works for part of each week with a hospital chaplain as a requirement for a course in pastoral care and counselling. In equipping lay people for pastoral care concurrent placements will obviously be the norm, where the focus of training may be the setting up of groups within congregations to undertake baptismal visits or to provide support for the bereaved.

Again both types of courses have their advantages. In the block placement the student can give undivided attention to the task in hand, being fully involved in all the activities of the placement without the problems of time clashes with college commitments. A further strength of the intern year in the US is that the student returns to seminary with a different perspective, and a fresh set of questions with which to struggle during the final period of academic work. The advantage of a concurrent placement is that there is (at least ideally) constant interaction between the work of ministry and the questions arising from that, and the academic pursuits of the theological college. In a concurrent placement it is important that good communication be maintained between college tutors and placement supervisors. When this is not attended to, one of two consequences may follow. On the one hand, the learner may hear contradictory messages concerning the relative importance of academic studies and practical experience; on the other hand, it has been not unknown for learners to play off one aspect of ministerial training against the other, as we saw in the section on 'Games' in the previous chapter.

*Parochial and non-parochial placements*

The normative arena of pastoral education is the local congregation. This somewhat bald statement can be justified, at least empirically, on the grounds that most of the recipients of pastoral training will exercise much of their subsequent ministry in and on behalf of the Church. This is not to deny that a great deal of pastoral care takes place outside ecclesiastical structures, by chaplains in institutions or by lay people within their secular vocations. It is simply to recognise that pastoral care is central to the life and ministry of the Church, which therefore in its most visible manifestation, the local congregation, must be an important locus of pastoral training. Placements in parochial settings will normally be 'in-role' placements and may be either 'block' or 'concurrent.'

In practice much of the creative development in pastoral education in the past fifty years has taken place in non-parochial settings, the Clinical Pastoral Education movement having taken root in general and psychiatric hospitals in North America. It is easy to see why this should have happened since the hospital arena can more readily fulfil the criteria for a good placement mentioned earlier in this chapter. The disadvantage of the hospital setting is that pastoral care may come to be understood in terms of the medical model of 'diagnosis/cure' which, as we have already seen, has been strongly criticised as inappropriate for ministry. Yet the recent burgeoning of interest in Theological Field Education which is largely parish-based owes a great deal to understanding of supervision developed in Clinical Pastoral Education.

## THE PRACTICALITIES OF CONSULTATION

Consultation and supervision are sometimes used interchangeably to describe the work of helping the helpers. We distinguish between them in this way: Supervision assumes that the supervisor is, at least in part, responsible for the work of the supervisee, whereas the consultant is not responsible for the work of the consultee. Consultants are responsible *to* rather than *for* their consultees.

### Characteristics of pastoral consultation

We have found the principles of mental health consultation as introduced by G. Caplan to be particularly helpful in defining the nature of pastoral consultation, and in providing some useful guidelines for consultants and those who come to them. We offer our adaptation of these as follows:

a) Pastoral consultation is a method of helping pastors, lay and clerical, with their pastoral work with individuals, groups and organisations.

b) The consultees' work, problems or issues must be defined by them, and if possible the focus clarified by them as well.

Parishioner-, client-, group- or organisation-centred focus.
Consultee-centred focus.

In Chapter 6 a client-centred focus in Peter's story would have attended to the two families, the Davidsons and the Smiths, an organisation focus would have attended to the children's ward and the chaplain's work within it, and a consultee focus would have concentrated on Peter's own role and experience.

c) The consultants have no management or professional responsibility for the outcome of their consultees' work. Consultants have no responsibility for changing or modifying the work or the practice of their consultees, and the latter have no need to accept or use the consultants' ideas or suggestions. This is the major difference between supervision, as we have presented it, and consultation.

d) The relationship of consultee and consultant is never hierarchical. They are equals who have different tasks to perform. According to Caplan,

> This is a situation that potentiates the influence of ideas. The freedom of the consultee to accept or reject what the consultant says enables him to take quickly as his own the ideas that appeal to him in his current situation.[5]

This is most easily achieved if consultees and consultants work in different places, parishes or institutions, and meet only and specifically for consultation. An unrealistic dependence on the consultant is then avoided, as it is if a consultant works with a number of consultees in a group. Some pastors intentionally consult with those of a non-religious or non-pastoral discipline, in order to gain a different perspective on their work.

e) The agenda for a consultation is always the responsibility of the consultees, and consultants work only with the issues and those aspects of them presented by the consultees. The aim is to help consultees improve their understanding of a current work problem, and to increase their capacity to cope with future problems of a similar kind.

f) The focus of consultation is always on the consultees' work and ministry, and not on the consultees themselves. Consultants in paying attention to the feelings and personal experience of their consultees will respect their privacy, and treat their personal experience in a special way, by exploring it in the form in which it has been displaced onto the consultees' work and ministry. Thus Mary was trying to help Peter acknowledge his identification with the 'Smiths' and the 'Davidsons'.

Pastoral consultation is most effective if it is practised within a structure which acknowledges the importance of these characteristics, not as rules to be enforced, but as guidelines to help consultees and consultants make the most of their own particular gifts and methods of working. There is no special magic or mystery to consultation of this kind; all pastors can offer one another something of this facility, within the limits of their experience and competence. As long as they are not led to exceed those limits or to stray too far from these guidelines, they will be offering something of considerable worth.

### Methods of consultation

a) Triads

In Chapter 6 we described in some detail a relatively simple way for pastors to offer consultation to one another. We favour triads or quartets rather than consulting in pairs if the consultation is to be mutual, as this offers the additional perspective of the observer to help identify the mirroring or reflection process which is so useful in providing understanding of the less conscious aspects of pastoral work.

b) Working individually with a consultant

Much of our discussion about supervision has concentrated on the work of individuals with their supervisor. Consultants can be used in much the same way, but with the essential difference that they have no professional or managerial responsibility for their consultees' work.

c) Group consultation

In Chapter 6 we mentioned the use of pastoral support and training groups as a method of consultation. This has many advantages as it provides pastors and other helpers with an opportunity to share their work in a secure environment, which, by its very nature, will often be able to re-present in the group many of the different aspects that play a part in the work of the participants. The simulation and role-play in Reg's story explicitly exploited this factor. At the same time it reinforces the corporate nature of pastoral care which has so often been over-individualised.

Of course groups need to find their own most effective ways of working, so that there is sufficient structure to contain the anxieties of the participants (rivalry and envy between members of the same professions can undermine the work of groups) and sufficient flexibility to allow for the different needs and learning styles of the participants. A group contract similar to the Learning Agreement in supervision is a good way of achieving some balance between structure and flexibility (see Appendix D). It is also important that groups are effectively led by those with experience in group work as well as in consultation. We have heard of a community psychiatrist combining with a hospital chaplain to organise a group for local clergy seeking to develop their expertise with members of their congregations, who were also served by the local mental health teams.[6] In another scheme, similarly paired leaders from pastoral and health or social service backgrounds were organised to lead a network of support and training groups for clergy and laity who wished to consult with one another about their pastoral work.[7] In this case the leaders of these groups meet regularly for supervision of their work in leaders' groups. An example of the kind of group contract which they devised appears in Appendix D.

Consultation, like supervision, is still relatively new to pastoral ministry. That is not to say that pastors have not consulted one another about many different things, but rather that the organisation of pastoral care has rarely been conceived of as part of an overall institutional plan for the Churches, and as central to their work for the kingdom of God. As we have seen, pastoral care is often fragmented and restricted to particular individuals and small groups. It offers some balm to the wounded of society, without questioning and exploring the nature of the wounding and its significance for us all. We believe that one of the major objectives of pastoral consultation and supervision is to help us see how the individual and the specific is a part of the whole, and how to treat it accordingly. Hopefully the growing practice and expertise of supervisors and consultants will help us towards a greater sense of the corporate nature of pastoral care, and our own place within it.

## Notes

1. Faber, H., *Pastoral Care in the Modern Hospital*, SCM 1971.
   Foskett, J. H., *Meaning in Madness*, SPCK 1984.
2. Dicks, R. R., *And Ye Visited Me*, New York: Harper and Bros 1939, p. 7.
3. Stott, P., *Milestones: the Diary of a Trainee G.P.*, Pan 1983, p. 159.
4. Courses in Supervision and Consultation are provided by The Chaplaincy Department, The Maudsley Hospital, Denmark Hill, London SE5 and The Westminster Pastoral Foundation, 23 Kensington Square, London W8. The Association for Pastoral Care and Counselling and the British Association for Counselling, 37a Sheep Street, Rugby CV21 3X have accreditation and recognition schemes for supervisors, lists of those accredited and recognised, codes of practice, etc.
5. Caplan, G., *The Theory and Practice of Mental Health Consultation*, New York: Basic Books 1970, p. 26.
6. Leishman, M., Unpublished Paper on Group Consultation at the Royal Infirmary, Edinburgh.
7. Southwark Diocesan Pastoral Care and Counselling Support and Training Groups.

# Learning Contract Form

The following is an example of a simple Learning Contract Form, in which we have used one of John's goals (see Chapter 3) to illustrate parts of the form (most contracts involve a number of goals relating to different objectives). Under 'Assessment' the student and supervisor can give a score (1 – 5) against each of the 'Methods', and then expand on this with 'Comments on the Assessment'.

STUDENT: John                     SUPERVISOR: Chaplain
PLACEMENT DETAILS: Geriatric ward in a hospital.
LEARNING GOAL 1: To learn to care for the elderly.

METHODS OF ACHIEVING GOAL          ASSESSMENT

                                Student    Supervisor

1. Visiting elderly patients on the wards and recording conversations with them, to be reviewed in supervision.              . . .        . . .
2. Observing how other professions care for the elderly, and discussing this with them.                            . . .        . . .
3. Exploring my own experience of elderly people and trying to understand how that has affected me.             . . .        . . .
4. Reading at least one book about the experience of being old.               . . .        . . .

COMMENTS ON THE ASSESSMENT

| Student | Supervisor |
|---|---|

1. Visited patients regularly each week, and formed a close relationship with two very different patients, one who was easy to get on with, and one who rejected me initially. I produced four verbatims of conversations.

2. I observed the way in which different nurses worked, how some would do everything for the patients and how others encouraged the patients to do things for themselves, so making them less dependent. I joined in a teaching session with the nurses about this.

3. I explored my own experience as a child in a household with two elderly people and recognised how that affected the way I relate instinctively to old people.

4. I read and wrote a book review of *The View in Winter* by R. Blythe.


FURTHER AIMS FOR STUDENT:

Gain more experience in either an old people's home, or through a psychogeriatric service within a hospital or in the community.
Read more widely and theologically about the subject.

# APPENDIX B

# Verbatim Form

CONFIDENTIAL: This verbatim is a confidential document.

PASTOR'S NAME:
DATE OF INTERVIEW:
NUMBER OF INTERVIEW:
INITIALS OF PARISHIONER/PATIENT:
LOCATION OF INTERVIEW:
LENGTH OF INTERVIEW:
SUPERVISOR'S NAME:

## 1. KNOWN FACTS:                Supervisor's Comments

*(Include all the known details about the person being interviewed—age, sex, religious affiliation, reason for interview etc. — the situation and the occasion of the interview.)*

## 2. BACKGROUND, OBSERVATIONS AND ASSUMPTIONS:

*(Include your plans and expectations for the interview, what you observed and felt as it began, the appearance of the person interviewed, etc.)*

## 3. DIALOGUE                Student's Comments

*(Record what you remember of the conversation as it happened, what you said and what the person you interviewed said, numbering each sequence.)*

*(Record here your thoughts and feelings, observations observations and intuitions.)*

159

## 4. ANALYSIS                    Supervisor's Comments

### 4.1 Person

(*Record here what you think the person was feeling and thinking during the interview, and how he/she is as a result of it*)

### 4.2 Pastor

(*Record what was happening to you during the interview, where you think you succeeded and/or failed in your offering of pastoral care.*)

### 4.3 Theological reflection

(*Record here the implicit and explicit beliefs and meanings expressed. Note any themes or associations with biblical or theological ideas. Discuss any ethical issues or dilemmas.*)

### 4.4 Future aims

(*Record here what you hope or intend to do next.*)

### 4.5 Why this conversation?

(*Record here why you chose to write up this conversation, and what you feel and think about it now.*)

# APPENDIX C

# Assessment and Evaluation Form

---

Assessment and evaluation can be done either in relation to the Learning Contract (see Appendix A), or on a form like this.

STUDENT:                    SUPERVISOR:

I have learnt the following about my identity and expertise as a pastor in relation to the following:

Supervisor's Comments

1. PARISHIONERS, PATIENTS, CLIENTS:


2. OTHER PROFESSIONS: (staff in a hospital, community workers etc.)


3. FELLOW STUDENTS:


4. MY SUPERVISOR:


MYSELF:


DD:

# Contract for a Pastoral Support and Training Group

―――――

*The aims of the group*

To provide the participants with opportunities to:

— share and explore their practice of pastoral care, and the effect that has on them and those for whom they care;
— encourage the development of each member's own pastoral identity;
— contribute to each member's understanding of working in and with a group of pastoral carers.

*Meetings*

The group meets for 90-minute sessions once a week for three terms of ten weeks per year.

*Confidentiality*

What is done and said within the group is held in trust by the group members.

*Joining and Leaving*

Groups work best when there is a high level of trust amongst the members. This is difficult to achieve if membership changes rapidly. New members to the group are invited only after discussion by the whole group, and when a member ha to leave a term's notice is to be given.

*Fees*

The group's expenses include administration, leaders supervisors' fees; these can be met from members' own and or from their church or institution's training fund

# Index